INTERNATIONAL REWARD AND RECOGNITION

Stephen J. Perkins

The Chartered Institute of Personnel and Development is the leading publisher of books and reports for personnel and training professionals, students, and all those concerned with the effective management and development of people at work.
For full details of all our titles, please contact the Publishing Department:
Tel: 020 8612 6204
E-mail: publish@cipd.co.uk

To view and purchase all CIPD titles:
www.cipd.co.uk/bookstore

For details of CIPD research projects:
www.cipd.co.uk/research

INTERNATIONAL REWARD AND RECOGNITION

Stephen J. Perkins

DEPARTMENT OF MANAGEMENT AND PROFESSIONAL DEVELOPMENT
LONDON METROPOLITAN UNIVERSITY

© Chartered Institute of Personnel and Development 2006

First published 2006
Reprinted 2006

Cover and text design by Sutchinda Rangsi-Thompson
Typeset by Paperweight
Printed in Great Britain by Antony Rowe

British Library Cataloguing in Publication Data
A catalogue record for this book is available from the British Library

ISBN   1 84398 176 9
ISBN-13   978 1 84398 176 3

Chartered Institute of Personnel and Development,
151 The Broadway, London SW19 1JQ

Tel: 020 8612 6200
Website: www.cipd.co.uk

Incorporated by Royal Charter. Registered charity no. 1079797.

CONTENTS

ACKNOWLEDGEMENTS

The CIPD would like to thank Professor Stephen Perkins, author of this report.

Thanks also go to Vice-President, International, Martin Ferber, and to previous Vice-Presidents, John Campbell, Bob McCall and Bob Morton for their support of this project.

Particular acknowledgement is due to Siobhan Cummins, European Managing Director ORC Worldwide, for organising and financing support for the survey exercise, and to Samantha Blackhurst, based in ORC Worldwide's New York offices, for the technical support and administrative management of the online data collection instrument.

Sincere thanks, too, are extended to Chris Asherson, John Brannigan, Sarah Charles, Richard Charlesworth, Richard Cook, Cecile de Calan, Tim Fevyer, Pat Fulker, Javier Goldsman, Anja Hanses, Karel Leeflang, Don Mackinlay, Phil Mills, Helen Murlis, Jean-Pierre Noel, Liz Spencer, Michael Reiff, Tracy Searl, N. Sundar, Phil Wills, Clive Wright and Vicky Wright. We are also very appreciative of members of the CIPD International and Reward Forums for their helpful input during the research, and of all those who responded to the survey.

LIST OF FIGURES AND TABLES

FOREWORD

The world has changed greatly since 1999 when the CIPD last examined reward and recognition issues in an international context. For instance, globalisation has caused most employers to face intense cost and quality competition. Organisations are increasingly focusing on performance and trying to ensure that employees are accountable and rewarded for their contribution. We are seeing a global pay-for-contribution approach emerge, if not for all employees, at least for middle and senior managers. Employers are examining new approaches to the mobilisation and deployment of talent as the cost and risk of moving employees around the planet increases.

Against this backdrop, the CIPD decided to commission research to establish how employers were responding to these and other global pressures and to offer support and guidance for practitioners grappling with these forces to develop a way to deliver competitive advantage for their employers. This research report is aimed at human resource practitioners operating internationally to provide them with the latest thinking on the range of options available to them in the development of a business-focused international compensation and benefits strategy.

The report is an integral part of research into international people management and development which includes a guide on international management development and a research report on international recruitment, selection and assessment. Combined together they provide practitioners, consultants and academics with a unique insight into international HR management and learning and development.

We hope you enjoy reading our report on reward and recognition issues in an international context.

Charles Cotton
CIPD Adviser, Reward

Frances Wilson
Manager, International, CIPD

INTERNATIONAL REWARD AND RECOGNITION

EXECUTIVE SUMMARY

Organisational leaders and their advisers are faced with evaluating alternative ideas and courses of action open to them, not just in the vacuum of their own corporate goals and environment. In the case of strategies for reward management, internationally diffused debates and the consequences of managerial choices form an additional spur to action.

There are many publications offering valuable checklists, for example, on what to do when planning to deploy employees on expatriate terms, or associated with the HR implications of multinational business acquisitions and joint ventures. And there are equally high-quality 'country guides' covering a range of issues associated with employing and deploying people. Management consultants provide clients with useful surveys enabling them to benchmark their practices against those reported in other organisations, both associated with international mobility and increasingly regarding reward management practices extended to employees in operations around the world. This CIPD publication – one of a series on international people management and development – adopts a different, though complementary, approach.

The report:

❖ describes and synthesises current ideas in the academic literature and related sources about the approaches open to multinational organisations in designing and managing employee reward systems

❖ uses the findings of research undertaken specifically for this publication to channel reflection on thinking and practice towards how international reward and recognition ideas are being interpreted and applied managerially.

Our ambition is to help users of this report to think systematically about the range of factors they should consider when designing and operating reward strategy – the questions they need to ask and the issues they need to bear in mind.

MANAGERIAL PRACTICE CONTINUITIES AND NEW DEVELOPMENTS

This report builds on an earlier guide on International Reward published in 1999. Back then, a significant emphasis on 'agency' was observable, manifested in the role accorded to 'global champions' (Perkins and Hendry, 2001). Accompanying this was the attempt corporately to engage senior managers in more 'federal behaviours' as organisations shifted towards a 'transnational' organisational model (Ghoshal and Bartlett, 1998), following a 'business streams' operating and financial control approach. In the current research, more structural factors have come into play.

Accountability of outcome – pragmatism in administration

There is an emphasis on 'accountability' (within prescribed organisational boundaries), limiting room for manoeuvre below the corporate level. Increasingly tight corporate governance standards appear to have strengthened corporate management resolve to offer new monitoring structures to co-ordinate what people do more prescriptively across multinational networks.

There also appears to be a greater pragmatism in cost management of the expatriate package, as organisations clarify:

❖ the need to integrate local leadership more effectively, rather than ignore the economic gap between long-term expatriate assignment terms and local compensation

❖ differentiation between groups of internationally mobile employees reflected in expectations and outcomes around reward determination. The overriding emphasis is on **performance contribution**. And the performance–reward link appears to be increasingly established not just at senior levels but through corporate pay systems that imply central control penetrating far more deeply into local operating hierarchies – at least at the level of corporate standard-setting.

Opportunism in multinational corporate knowledge management

Agency is sometimes perceived in terms of the demand to generate and transfer knowledge around organisational networks. Structure can be perceived in the attempt to standardise the terms on which the employment relationship is governed, despite apparent scope for individuals to 'flex' detailed application: a 'mass customisation' orientation. Where new HR IT is introduced, the question is whether the policy to standardise reward systems is the driver or the need for policy standardisation to fit in with the new IT system. Perhaps a symbiotic relationship exists in which each is influenced by the other. And the overall influences could be cost reduction through the streamlining and reduction of physical HR support needs (especially those employed in an administrative capacity), while at the same time enabling enhanced central surveillance and control of devolved managerial responsibility.

The implication is increasing centralisation – but there is still a choice between unitary strategy and pluralistic adaptation across countries, and opportunism is seen as operating in practice. This is particularly noticeable in comments about the influences on transnational reward determination, where a hybrid approach orientation is perceptible in views expressed by practitioners.

Networked relations – local/global skill sets and market pressures

Expatriation continues to be used as part of the mobilisation of corporate knowledge and for the supervision of local operations/ management, but the emphasis is more on performance that can be measured as 'adding value' across global networks, raising issues for expatriate–local employee relationships, including reward comparability factors.

And finally, a continuing problem that organisation respondents say they are wrestling with relates to certain market pressures in acquiring key skills and having performance-based relations where consistency of approach to key groups is aimed for. This is notable particularly in transatlantic reward management relations.

INTRODUCTION

❖ **Corporate governance issues more explicitly connect with people performance and reward management factors.**

❖ **Mobilising knowledge across international networks implies continuity in expatriation terms but managed differently than in the past.**

❖ **New organisation and employment forms raise issues around network relationships with implications for how people view reward and recognition.**

The research reported here evaluates current influences on international reward management strategy, and analyses qualitative and quantitative evidence to interpret what multinational reward designers say they are doing in practice.

This research updates and builds on a similar project carried out seven years ago (Perkins and Hendry, 1999a). New primary research is presented on practitioners' perceptions of reward and recognition management in a variety of multinational organisations. Academic commentary is drawn on to shape and make sense of the data, with an emphasis on making theoretical literature accessible to reflexive practitioners who wish to think systematically about international people management and the space in which employee performance and reward management interacts. The overriding aim is thus to create actionable knowledge.

RESEARCH QUESTIONS AND STRUCTURE OF THE REPORT

The report is organised into four main parts, using evidence drawn from a literature review, survey responses from a sample of multinational HR specialists, and qualitative interviews with a group of senior HR people in significant organisations across a variety of sectors (see Appendix).

We anticipate that users of this publication may face questions that include:

❖ How are multinational managements structuring and managing organisations, and what are the consequences for managing employee reward dependent on the organisational model being followed?

❖ To what extent is the mobilisation of knowledge to secure effective multinational organisation something that involves the physical mobilisation of people, and

what are the reward management consequences and options for addressing them?

❖ How can performance management be co-ordinated across geographical areas

❖ Is the world of reward management more convergent or does practice for different workforce segments and in different locations continue to diverge?

❖ Can we transplant the substance and process of reward management without modification when developing the organisation's operations internationally?

❖ How do reward practitioners interpret the variety of influences on how they choose to set a strategic course?

❖ What are the norms prescribed by academics for securing organisational effectiveness? What priority do multinational managements place on these and their practical application?

❖ What are the differences in business system characteristics, and what account does commentary and recorded practice take of these in approaching international reward management?

❖ Are there differences in perceptions of what people say they value, and how managers prefer to manage?

CONTEXT FOR INTERNATIONAL REWARD AND RECOGNITION

The context for international employee reward and recognition is one of continuous change. Since this report's predecessor was published, not only has the so-called 'war for talent', to secure and retain the most able and experienced workforce members, intensified (Michaels, Handfield-Jones, and Axelrod, 2001), a variety of major developments have exacerbated the problems multinational employers face in motivating staff to meet strategic business goals. At the head of the list, tensions and concerns about security have been amplified – in particular, following high profile terrorism across national boundaries (Turner and Newman, 2005). Regionalised political tensions may place western expatriates at risk (eg the attacks by 'ethnic militants' on oil platforms in Nigeria reported by Ashby, 2006).

CORPORATE GOVERNANCE AND GLOBAL COMPETITIVE DEMANDS

There has been an explosion of regulatory interest among governments and finance capital investors associated with the effective and transparent governance of business corporations. The UK chairman of Shell told a CIPD audience in April 2004 that he perceived these issues to be at the heart of performance management (*People Management*, 2004, p7).

The generation and transfer of knowledge (Goodherham and Nordhaug, 2003) is central to the achievement of corporate governance aims in contemporary multinationals – not simply for-profit enterprises, but also agencies and institutions accountable to politicians or charitable trustees. And

> ...global industries and other international arrangements have become the main source of pressure for business activities all around the world. Global competition and markets have become the main driving force behind strategy and structure of organisations.
>
> (Farashahi, Hafsi and Molz, 2005, p15).

At the level of operational strategy and its interface with HRM and reward and recognition strategies, investment in reward and recognition may be tied to sourcing, retaining, and mobilising individuals and groups employed by the organisation with the capability to generate and network transnational knowledge cost-effectively.

EXPATRIATION

The requirement for international employee mobility continues as new multinationals emerge and mature transnational corporations reorganise their operations – not only in the commercial sector, but also in not-for-profit and non-governmental organisations. Plans to preserve or increase internationally mobile employee numbers were reported by most respondents from large multinationals in North America, Europe, Asia Pacific, Latin America and Middle East/Africa questioned in a recent survey (Mercer HRC, 2005). However, companies indicate shifting practices in how mobility is managed, with increasing use of short-term expatriation over traditional assignments.

OUTSOURCING AND OFF-SHORING

'Outsourcing' and 'off-shoring' of business operations from developed economies to those undergoing development and transformation increase (*Economist*, 2004). While these trends may lessen the burden of expatriation (although off-set globally by developments noted above), they raise new issues for organisations seeking to invest reward and recognition budgets in ways that are likely to enhance employee motivation to perform efficiently and effectively to westernised governance standards.

SUMMARY

Each of the four chapters that follow this introduction is based on

- ❖ making theories to underpin international reward and recognition strategy and practice *accessible* to decision takers and their advisers

- ❖ findings from research on international reward management practice undertaken to inform the report, balanced with other empirical data

- ❖ offering pointers to action in weighing the choices and consequences (Perkins and Shortland, 2006) associated with international reward systems design and management.

INTERNATIONAL REWARD AND RECOGNITION IN CONTEXT

❖ **Meanings attached to employee reward and recognition.**

❖ **The complex nature of *international* employee recognition and reward.**

❖ **Strategic issues to help guide reflection when designing and operating reward systems to match organisational aims.**

The design and maintenance of an organisation's employee reward system represents 'a critical responsibility' of HR managers. And 'the conduct of international business makes this responsibility much more complex and difficult' (Briscoe and Schuler, 2004; p305).

The claim begs the question of what employee reward and recognition is. It also calls for some statement of context. Notions of reward and recognition must be located as part of a system that is organised and operated to manage investment in employees to pursue organisational objectives. A discussion of definitions and context will set the scene for those who are faced with choices about employee reward determination associated with international activities.

DEFINING 'EMPLOYEE REWARD'

Employee compensation, remuneration, reward – an interchangeable meaning is attributed to these terms in this report – has been defined (Milkovich and Newman, 1989; p3) as:

> *all forms of financial returns and tangible services and benefits employees receive.*

Such forms of 'extrinsic reward', representing 'a central pillar of the employment relationship' (Kessler, 2005; p316), can be distinguished from environmental factors, development opportunities and other intrinsic phenomena associated with work and employment.

And 'extrinsic reward' can, in turn, be understood as embracing aspects of the 'effort–reward bargain' (Kessler, 2001; p208) that translate into material factors such as pay, perks, paid holiday, insurances (for example, related to healthcare), share-based reward and other long-term benefits (notably, retirement pensions). Milkovich and Newman (1989) argue that other forms of employee recognition such as verbal acknowledgement of

outstanding work, promotions, and individual feelings of accomplishment should be co-ordinated with compensation wherever possible, perhaps under a 'total reward' system approach.

Valuing the employment relationship

Work performed in return for extrinsic rewards is the foundation of the employment relationship (Rubery and Grimshaw, 2003). This notion of an economic exchange implies recognition of a contribution by an employee. From the employee's perspective, value may be viewed in terms of recognition of his or her personal skills and abilities, reflecting prior attainment, which he or she is willing to put to work for an employer. Influencing that perspective will be views of fairness and justice in the distribution of rewards.

Managers have a stake in employee reward determination, viewed from two perspectives. First, pay and other employee benefits constitute a major expense. Second, managers regard reward as a source of influence on employee work attitudes and behaviours. This raises the question of the extent to which managers are able to control the costs of rewarding employees and to influence employee motivation to perform work tasks while demonstrating the desired attitudes and behaviours. Wright (2004) reports evidence that the sophistication of managerial approaches to reward determination tends to increase with the scale of operations – reflecting the resources to fund the HR management architecture to administer employment arrangements.

MANAGING REWARD INTERNATIONALLY

A case can be made that the design and management of reward systems is complex and open to contested viewpoints, amplified by Briscoe and Schuler's (2004) claim that designing and administering reward internationally adds further complexity and difficulty.

Located in a transnational employment systems context, the contingencies associated with active 'reward management' initiatives might include:

❖ relations between the strategic aims set by corporate management for the multinational

❖ an appraisal of the relationship between corporate policies and practices for determining rewards dependent on the job, the person, and the performance of employees across a variety of locations, segmented by geography or occupational category or other material factor

❖ an account of the 'human capital' perspective – the implied or express needs and priorities of individuals and groups engaged to work for the organisation.

Continuities and differences

So what is the same and what is different about international reward and recognition strategy, compared with what is known and practised by managers in their domestic operations in the British Isles? On one level, nothing at all. If the organisation is a multinational operating in the UK and Ireland, the policies and systems may well be 'foreign' anyway. And given the prevailing ideas about what constitutes good practice in people management, much of what is done in setting and maintaining the reward and other ways of recognising people engaged in an employment relationship reflects a non-domestic view of the world.

Differences arising from multinational organisation directly impacting on international HR management generally, and the design and administration of reward systems in particular, are the *context* and the *knowledge* required to purposefully manage the effort–reward nexus when not just bounded by one domestic environment (Dowling *et al*, 1999). Transnational reward strategies are required for application across three national or country categories: the parent country where the organisation is usually headquartered; the host country where a subsidiary may be located; and other countries that might be the source, for example, of employees, finance, or research development (Scullion, 2005).

Dowling and Welch (2004) list six core international HR management themes, adapted below to account for the varieties of workers and their employment settings to differentiate international reward management from the domestic people management sub-category:

❖ a wider range of activities to scope and administer reward policy

❖ the need for a broader perspective

❖ in the case of expatriates, more involvement in employees' personal lives

❖ responsiveness to changes in the market value of international workforce members and their performance alignment with evolving international strategy

❖ higher risk exposure in terms of economic and political environmental factors

❖ more external influences.

The complexities of operating transnational employee reward systems across a variety of cultural and institutional settings, involving different national categories of workers, means that managers have to become knowledgeable in how to access and interpret conditions within a range of national employment systems. This knowledge must be partnered with how to manage across and within the countries in which the company operates while supporting corporate strategic aims and objectives. It follows that underestimating the complexities involved is likely to lead to underperformance (Scullion, 2005). The common worldview of organisations as goal-directed, unified, rational actors may be open to question: multinationals may be regarded as sites within which multiple social actors, from a diversity of backgrounds, interact – with distinctive views on how to manage.

> 'The key message is that...reward management principles and practices are socially constructed.'

Following this, managers in the multinational organisation also bring their own interests in career progression and development to the ways they interpret attempts to transplant corporate routines. In evaluating the influences on international reward strategies it is worth giving some attention to the sequences multinationals go through, reflecting the calculations by particular corporate managements of different sorts of internationalisation within their product markets and sectors, and the role which network relationships play in this process (Morgan, 2001; p6). The key message is that, as with the multinational organisation itself, reward management principles and practices are socially constructed.

The contingencies argument can be developed further to pose questions about how multinational managements prioritise between: corporate strategy goals, adaptation to business systems, and responsiveness to human capital:

❖ Is universal application of a global (headquarters-designed) approach to reward and recognition management to be pursued as a necessary reflection of corporate organisation strategy?

❖ Or do policy-makers acknowledge a need to adapt universal reward management norms to accommodate different norms and associated values encountered in the multiplicity of operating environments around the world?

❖ And to what extent do human capital priorities and market bargaining power feature in corporate choices when setting and administering reward systems?

❖ Is the notion of an effort–reward bargain as a dynamic phenomenon such that, in practice, reward management strategy is emergent rather than predetermined? Do decision-makers act opportunistically to secure the match between the potentially competing contingencies identified above, settling on a hybrid reward system?

The issues for corporate reward management policy-makers and their advisers become clearer when focusing attention on particular groups. There is an extensive literature on approaches to setting the terms and conditions applied to people who are assigned by their employer beyond their country of origin (expatriates). While the need for transnational mobility of individuals (and their family members) gives rise to special considerations, the underlying principles governing international employee reward systems are, however, generally the same across all employee groups in the multinational.

Times change, and considerations of corporate governance require organisation leaders to be increasingly alert to the need for investment in the people they employ to serve the organisation's needs to be cost-effective. Organisations can afford only to pay for the kinds of skills and performance levels judged to make the investment return commensurate with the measures applied to evaluate the effectiveness of the organisation as a whole. When commentators relate employee reward management initiatives to 'recruit, retain, motivate', the intended point is that organisations competing to survive and prosper in a competitive environment subject to economic 'globalisation' must direct the resources available to reward and recognise people who realise the potential to support the organisation management's corporate purpose.

Unilever, a branded goods company employing 234,000 people in around 100 countries around the world, has been undergoing a major corporate transformation initiative. Thinking through the meaning of active management of the effort–reward nexus, the accent is on enhanced focus and transnational integration, while remaining sensitive to the contextual variety impacting on the substance of employee recognition across the geographies in which the group company operates. Underlining the more integrated approach within the HR function, talent management, organisational effectiveness, learning, and reward have been combined in one team to enable specialists 'to look at the tools we have and pick a match to take people through the knowledge'.

Attention is being focused on 'helping people understand how they create value', a managerial intervention that is seen as an important driver of corporate performance. Reward system architects do not anticipate changes to the reward system design. Instead, the emphasis is on improving its execution, aligned with the new corporate strategic priorities. The challenge is seen as one of 'articulating value creation as something that is relevant' to people, accommodating variety in economic conditions affecting regional operations. While growth opportunities are 'amazing' in emerging markets, employee opinion indicates that rewards require tailoring using a 'currency key' that, without inflating results, enables achievements relative to the fluctuations in monetary values to reflect substantive achievements. By contrast, in more 'mature'

economies, such as those of western Europe, the managerial task is perceived as one of 'maintaining momentum' through making the achievement of targets associated with *retaining* profitable market share 'as relevant, as sexy, as growing 20%' (as might be possible in markets to the east such as Poland and Russia).

You work with some really good strategic financial planning people who understand the people well, and you work with inspired business leaders, and get them to say 'These are achievable targets,' presenting it in a way that says, 'Guys, we can make this and we can get top-notch.' Helping them understand what 'better' looks like is pretty important.

To match a corporate strategy intended to capitalise more effectively on corporate brands than may have been the case in the past, a new dimension has been added to Unilever's 'talent management listing process'. The intention is to integrate the identification of high potential employees with increased 'performance accountability'. The incentive management system has been adapted to recognise corporately aligned performance in ways that differentiate the distribution of extrinsic rewards. This initiative also represents a break with past practice, where the accent was on consistency in applying market-leading levels of reward.

SITUATING REWARD AND RECOGNITION WITHIN MULTINATIONAL MANAGEMENT PRACTICE

The most crucial of the many challenges faced by managers of multinational companies is the generation and transfer of knowledge across national settings, organisations and networks. This is not just our view, but it is a view shared by many of our fellow international management scholars. Significantly it is also the view of virtually all the international managers with whom we have spoken in the past ten years. Among other things, it influences the choice of organisational structure, the choice of human resource management system and the degree and type of expatriation.

(Goodherham and Nordhaug, 2003)

International activities are important to corporate well-being. And the *ideas* that managers are exposed to about how to run enterprises are increasingly international in character. Once, non-domestic subsidiaries may have been regarded as of limited importance, or at least there was an acceptance that the polycentric (Perlmutter, 1969) complexities of managing international operations inhibited corporate leaders from getting involved much beyond the appointment of (generally expatriate) leaders and passive monitoring of subsidiary performance against high-level financial commitments.

Transnational mobility has become a dynamic issue, no longer limited to the deployment of headquarters expatriates. Increasing competition in the global market can tempt business organisations to focus exclusively on fewer stakeholders. However, research such as that undertaken by Hillman and Keim (2001, cited in Mamman and Rees, 2005) investigating 500 firms indicates that effective stakeholder management can lead to improved shareholder value.

Reward interventions to support global knowledge management

In the 'knowledge economy', organisations do not only compete on their ability to mobilise the knowhow and matched resources to succeed across settings, organisations and networks (Goodherham and Nordhaug, 2003). Multinational success is also dependent on the speed and ease with which valuable knowledge is disseminated throughout the organisation (Gourlay, 2006).

As the Unilever case illustrates, strategic decision-making in international employee reward management can be viewed as dependent on the relationship between mobilising ideas and experience and the needs and possibilities of recognising people in systematic ways for their contribution. And the consequence of pressure to exploit global 'brand equity' and other forms of knowledge-based corporate assets is a far closer interest by headquarters leaderships in the detail of value creation processes in local operations. It follows that a critical task for top management is to structure the relationship between headquarters and subsidiaries (Hong Chung *et al*, 2006). If solving the transnational 'knowledge management' problem while synchronising subsidiary behaviour and performance becomes a central integrating function in the multinational, active HR management implies aligning HR management with organisational strategy. Structuring and administering complementary processes underpinning the multinational reward management system together form a core feature of that key corporate imperative.

The standardising potential of pay in systems of corporate control

Vernon draws attention to the strategic opportunities when regarding pay as a managerial resource in multinational organisations that has more 'standardisation' potential than other aspects of HR management due to 'the relative simplicity of administering pay across national borders' (2006, p217). Multinational managements have come under increasing pressure not only to secure and apply the knowledge needed to compete across worldwide markets for goods and services. The globalisation of capital markets, including creating a market in firms traded on international stock exchanges (Grahl, 2002, cited by Perkins, 2003), places pressure on organisations to prioritise the demands of financial shareholders. Standardisation in approaches to the effort–reward bargain therefore reflects not just a focus on knowledge generation and its multinational transfer. Such initiatives may also demonstrate the attempt to increase corporate control over devolved managerial practice across

transnational operations – in particular, to support shareholder value-maximisation-based corporate governance.

> 'The globalisation of capital markets...places pressure on organisations to prioritise the demands of financial shareholders.'

While highlighting its strategic potential, Vernon (2006) counsels that the unthinking application of western reward management principles is to be avoided. Multi-local institutional factors must be systematically appraised and managed before supposedly universal reward solutions are applied. Also, although it is possible administratively to enact changes initiated by the corporate centre, reorienting workforce expectations offers a more complex managerial challenge.

Universal 'best practice' or culturally sensitive tailoring?

In the literature on international organisations, a dichotomy exists surrounding notions of headquarters control versus the perceived need to adapt strategies for directing operations to fit the circumstances prevailing in a range of cultural settings. Mainstream ideas on how to lead and manage organisations tend to reflect the prevailing international consensus on best practice standards (Smith and Meiksins, 1995). Such ideas are a reflection of the environment they have emerged in – the question is whether or not such ideas can be freely transplanted across national borders. But slavish adaptation in compliance with perceived local culture, custom and related institutional factors may be unacceptable to multinational managements trying to sustain the strategic approach in pursuit of corporate aims. Corporate managers need thus to balance the competing demands of global best practice and local best fit.

And the culture factor is not one simply limited to geo-ethnic phenomena. In strong internal cultures that have socialised employees and operational managers to define the effort–reward nexus in particular ways it may take time for stakeholders to accept the legitimacy of an alternative point of view. In multinational IT company **Hewlett-Packard**, recalibration of the employment culture formerly known as 'the HP-way' to 'the plus HP-way', combining not just rationalisation of workforce numbers but also reduction in employee costs (pay freezes and bonus-level cutbacks), was greeted initially by employees in the Europe, Middle East and Africa region with a sense of denial. Externally, changes at top management level were recognised as the trigger for driving through 'efficiencies', leading to fundamental changes in the relationship between the organisation and its workforce. A reward specialist we interviewed highlighted a gap between the stock market perspective and the one held by many internal stakeholders. The external viewpoint had been the more accurate assessment of the changes taking place. Internally, given a long-standing employment experience perceived as 'They *really* look after you', people were not expecting transformation in the substance of corporate management actions hard-wired to pay.

> *There was a real mismatch between the stated values and the behaviours. And that kind of discrepancy*

between what you're saying and what you're doing creates huge problems for managers. They were starting to complain that 'We're saying one thing and doing another.' When we fed that issue back up the organisation, the message we got back was 'the business reality' – which is fair, which is correct. But that business reality, which is about cost minimisation, is not what the words were around our programmes. It's clear that the Company can act in a new way before it starts to talk in a new way. This change that the Company is going through is adjusting to that and trying to start to make the words match the actions.

Business adaptation, managerial style and reward bundle definition

While ultimately as 'hard-headed' in business terms, the HP approach can be contrasted with an apparently more evolutionary management style demonstrated in another case company. The management of the confectionery and soft drinks group of companies **Cadbury Schweppes**, employing 55,000 people in 35 countries, has had a tradition of strong corporate values stretching back two centuries. However, to meet the demands of contemporary Anglo-American corporate governance, corporate management is unequivocal about being 'fundamentally performance-oriented'.

We believe in justice and fairness and we have not fundamentally changed our character in 200 years. I would say: 'basically, different company, same values'. And those have obviously been modernised: performance is key – in terms of individuals, teams, functions, businesses, regions: the whole Group.

The working definition underscoring reward is that of a bundle of programmes intended to reinforce and to drive a perception, in the words of a corporate reward strategist, that the task is to give people employed throughout the group company's operations 'the opportunity to do great jobs in a great environment and deliver very high-quality personal and business results.' A guiding principle at corporate level is also 'to provide the right level of incentive and overall reward to get quality people to come and join us and stay with us'. This interpretation suggests that, as argued by Milkovich and Newman (1989), management perceives reward as a source of managerially controlled influence. And corporately, the exportability of reward programmes appears to have been subject to some recent re-evaluation – that is, processes that 'travel' across international borders have been examined as to whether they are governance processes or whether they are 'the way we do things' processes.

Even though we have a matrix structure, which is not that simple sometimes, particularly dealing with human resource matters, we are great believers now in 'Let's try and keep it simple.' We do believe that if we can get everybody going in the same direction using the same processes, then we'll have a very successful business model going forward. By the same processes, I don't mean necessarily using exactly the same combination of people processes and technology, but using what I call a comparative advantage type of approach. This means using the mix best suited to the economic circumstances of a particular business or a particular country. By the same token, I would hope to drive those reward processes and programmes that have 'legs' internationally through the businesses far more strongly than I could do so, say, five or six years ago.

CONCLUSIONS

Simplification and standardisation in designating the substance and process of international employee reward management is an emergent theme, both in the literature and in the views of practitioners interviewed for this report. The implications of this for designing and then managing the effort–reward nexus transnationally are developed in greater detail in Chapters 2 and 3, taking account also of the continued controversy surrounding notions of organisation and HR management convergence or divergence. However, an ambition to reduce complexity (whether in the constitution of terms recognising international mobility of employees and their families or in the tolerance for exceptions to the principle of matching extrinsic reward to the person and his or her performance contribution) does not imply a smooth passage to outcome.

Key points for practitioners

❖ When thinking about employee reward, remember that managerial aims and initiatives form only one side of the effort–reward bargain struck between the parties to the employment relationship.

❖ The same considerations apply whether employee reward is viewed managerially as a cost or as a source of influence.

❖ Associated with this reasoning, an examination of the interplay between efficiency and effectiveness considerations on the one hand, and on the other hand, perceptions of equity – however the parties to the employment relationship choose to define this notion across national and organisational boundaries – merits attention.

❖ When seeking to capitalise on the theoretical prospect to standardise pay systems, corporate policy-makers need to evaluate the extent to which they expect to transplant a common set of reward management principles and practices across a diverse array of geographies.

❖ The choice of retaining or rejecting 'the job' as the basic building-block in valuing work, or focusing on the relative worth of individuals and groups employed by organisations, also faces international reward decision-makers.

❖ If considering a shift to pay for performance, consequences must be weighed in terms of:

　❖ the capacity of managers in different employment systems to co-ordinate a pay-for-performance system competently and credibly, where input and output factors are likely to interact in complex ways

　❖ the willingness of employee groups socialised within different traditions to offer discretionary effort motivated by an offer that introduces a level of risk associated with their extrinsic reward

　❖ the extent to which the emphasis is placed on individuals isolated from the collective context in which value is generated within organisations.

❖ Identify the scope to communicate the effort–reward bargain in ways that enable employees to understand how they create value, while moderating the influences of extraneous factors that can distort performance–pay alignment – for example, currency volatility.

❖ Give attention to the role of reward management within initiatives to manage knowledge mobilisation across transnational networks at the core of multinational business strategy.

❖ Exercise sensitivity when instituting organisation-wide changes driven by contemporary competitive conditions so as to accommodate long-standing organisational cultural norms and values in order to support the sustainability of widespread stakeholder commitment.

CREATING A STRATEGY FOR INTERNATIONAL REWARD AND RECOGNITION

2

- ❖ **Choices by multinational managements in designing international reward and recognition arrangements.**

- ❖ **Alignment between these decisions and corporate strategy, transnational operating conditions, or a combination of these.**

- ❖ **Reported trends underpinning strategy, structure, and international reward design.**

- ❖ **Pointers to stimulate practitioner thinking on reported institutional factors affecting practice among multinationals originating in the US, Europe and Japan.**

OBJECTIVES UNDERPINNING INTERNATIONAL REWARD STRATEGY DESIGN

CIPD Assistant Director General, Duncan Brown, has argued that while it may seem 'blindingly obvious', given the mass of factors decision-makers and their advisers have to weigh up, a first step in designing a reward strategy is 'to arm yourself with a clear set of objectives' (2001; p110). To collect data on creating a strategy for international reward and recognition, a survey was undertaken specifically for this report in which respondents were asked about the influences they perceived as focusing their design choices.

In summer 2005, HR specialists in mainly European multinationals (see the Appendix for a more detailed methodology) were provided with a range of options that indicate whether a logic of a 'one-organisation, one global reward system', is being pursued to generate and mobilise knowledge across corporate networks, and to deliver maximum shareholder value. Alternatively, respondents were able to offer answers suggesting a strategy of adaptation informing reward design and implementation, reflecting a national culture logic, influenced by the multiplicity of ways operations and workforces were being managed.

Analysis of the data set provides a picture of opportunism and experimentation – a result broadly in line with earlier research undertaken by American academics (Bloom *et al*, 2003). This is detailed below and illustrated with a set of figures summarising the position. This material is then complemented by comparisons with previous studies.

Integrating reward and corporate strategy

Asked for their views on whether the priority was to integrate the reward system with corporate strategy for the multinational

(Figure 1 on page 10), 84% said it was (Figure 1a). But when the same respondents were asked whether they tended to adapt their reward system to the local host context, 62% still claimed it as the priority (Figure 1b). And when asked about whether a globally integrated approach would be preferred, 78% of respondents said 'Yes' (Figure 1c).

The findings can be read as implying indecision among survey participants, as though there is no strategy at all. However, if we adopt an emergent strategy definition (Whittington, 2000), the findings may well support the proposition that multinational managements will vary their approach based on the limitations and opportunities particular circumstances afford. Practice among survey respondents appears to be a blend of managerial styles, as multinational managements act opportunistically in seeking to apply reward management aligned with corporate strategy, while manoeuvring around the various host contingencies as they are encountered from place to place and sector to sector across employment systems.

Globalisation and reward strategy design

The reported approaches followed by multinational reward architects can be interpreted as strategic reactions to perceived opportunities and threats of 'globalisation' (Bloom *et al*, 2003).

Some commentators argue that financial rewards are highly sensitive to change, politically and socially. A national culture logic follows as the preferred multinational reward strategy design influence. As organisations expand their operations across national borders, they respect the comparative cultural and institutional settings they plan to employ people in. Managers are expected to conform or adapt to the deterministic or constraining force of culture (Bloom *et al*, 2003; p1351), subordinating

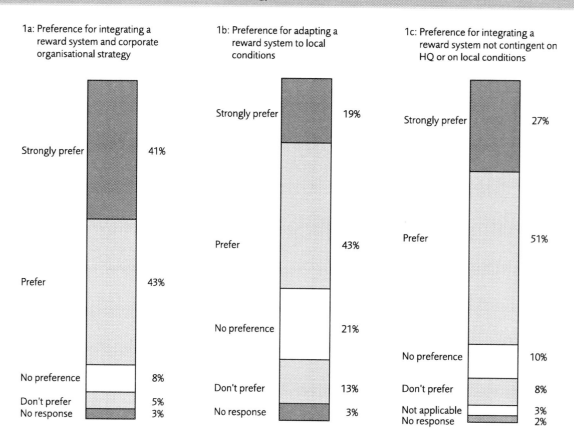

Figure 1 ❖ **Preferences for international reward strategy**

1a: Preference for integrating a reward system and corporate organisational strategy

Strongly prefer — 41%
Prefer — 43%
No preference — 8%
Don't prefer — 5%
No response — 3%

1b: Preference for adapting a reward system to local conditions

Strongly prefer — 19%
Prefer — 43%
No preference — 21%
Don't prefer — 13%
No response — 3%

1c: Preference for integrating a reward system not contingent on HQ or on local conditions

Strongly prefer — 27%
Prefer — 51%
No preference — 10%
Don't prefer — 8%
Not applicable — 3%
No response — 2%

managerial initiatives to meet corporate priorities to overarching local environmental considerations.

However, there is evidence that multinational managements are choosing to pursue a corporate alignment objective. An imperative to generate and mobilise knowledge across multinational networks implies that multinational decision-makers should match the employee reward system to the organisation's corporate strategy, culture, and managerial structures. From this perspective, environmental contingencies are subordinated to the imperative of adapting to, exploiting, and influencing the organisational context for competitive advantage. Reward strategy should support and enhance corporate objectives and the core competencies intended to achieve them (Bloom *et al*, 2003).

CIPD survey respondents indicated that the predominant sources of ideas about how to design a reward strategy to support international operations are management consultants (38%) and other multinational organisations (33%). Although 'what we've always done' is cited in 14% of cases, given the externally-oriented source of practice drivers, experimentation with various approaches does not seem surprising. And while 'national culture' logic may influence practice to an extent – employee expectations cited by only 6% of respondents – benchmarking shows that a preference for corporate alignment suggests convergence trends in pursuit of 'global' reward strategy. See Figure 2 (opposite).

In order to decide which approach is fit for purpose in the particular situation, it could be helpful for international reward

designers to reflect on their reaction to the following statements, based on their assessment of operational conditions:

❖ Considerations external to the organisation, and largely beyond management's reach (cultural forces mediated through institutions such as management federations, state agencies and trade unions), are dominant.

❖ Reward system design and operation is amenable to managerial control, so that the dominant organisation context will enable managerial action to bend environmental conditions to prescribed corporate purposes.

A matrix to inform decision-making

Bloom *et al* (2003) conducted case study research with five multinationals in a variety of business sectors to see how managers responded to the local conformance and strategic alignment pressures. Similar to the CIPD survey findings, their conclusion was that both conformance *and* alignment seem to co-exist in managerial thinking as both competing and complementary factors influencing employee reward management practice. Though claiming to be acting strategically, managers acted as 'pragmatic experimentalists' (Bloom *et al*, 2003; p1363), crafting the detail of reward systems around constraints encountered in local host environments, while remaining as consistent as possible with the intentions of corporate policy direction.

Figure 2   Sources of ideas on international reward and recognition strategy

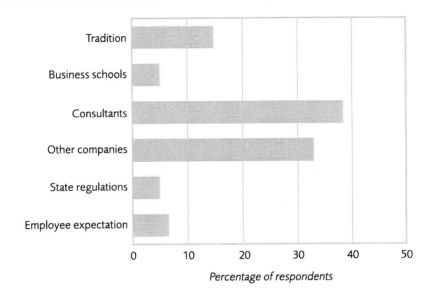

Percentage of respondents

Table 1   Context-related multinational reward management factors

	Conform	Avoid	Resist
Adapters	generally	where possible	rarely
Exporters	rarely	generally	if cost-effective
Globalisers	if necessary	sometimes	where feasible

Source: (based on) Bloom, Milkovich and Mitra (2003) 'International compensation', *International Journal of Resource Management*, 14: 1350–67.

The insight from the analysis is that the degree of variation in contextual factors *between and within* local host contexts rather than just the type of host contexts (cultural norms, economic conditions, regulatory pressures and so on) may be what matters most when multinational managements consider how to balance corporate versus host influences on reward strategy design.

Managerial styles associated with international reward design principles can be audited in terms of proximity to an 'adapter' (localiser), 'exporter' (one-world strategist), or 'globaliser' (integrater) orientation. Alternative managerial priorities can also be discerned between conformance to the local context, avoiding compliance as far as possible, or mounting a campaign of active resistance. The category framework summarised in Table 1 can be used to prompt systematic reflection on where multinational managements wish to situate their design choices, after weighing corporate priorities against intelligence on the local situation.

❖ *Adapters* tend to apply a 'multi-local' approach to product market competitive strategy and reward management (Bradley *et al*, 1999), matching the approach to most or all of

the local contexts they operate in. Scope for scale economies and best practice sharing is inhibited. At worst, the approach can fan the flames of turf wars, not only between business units and countries but also between operating units and corporate policy-shapers.

❖ *Exporters* adopt a control regime strongly aligned to corporate headquarters, with little interaction between subsidiaries, assuming that what works at headquarters can be force-fitted to satisfy reward arrangements everywhere. While expatriate managers feel at home administering policies wherever they are deployed, the approach can lead to resource-wasting attempts to change host contexts.

❖ *Globalisers* gather managerial practices (including those related to employee reward and recognition) that seem to work best from any and all locations and integrate them for application across all organisational units worldwide.

The approach is, of course, heavily dependent on co-operation between business units, creating network dependencies, and it risks a chaotic 'cobbled together' outcome unless carefully managed (Bloom *et al*, 2003).

❖ *Conformance* means adjusting reward system design and management when forces in the host location make it necessary, with the result that multinationals in the same location tend simply to adopt one another's practices, limiting the scope for differentiation in their reward proposition.

❖ *Avoidance* tactics may involve the introduction of buffers that help the organisation to limit the level of reward management compliance with local host contexts, sometimes just ignoring the contextual factors. For example, while needing people to work in a location, they may decide not to employ them directly there, contracting with them via a 'virtual office' somewhere nearby that is perceived as more accommodating, but deploying these workers for extended periods to the place where the work is really needed.

❖ *Resistance* may equally be premised on forestalling compliance with the local contextual conditions. However, unlike avoidance tactics, resistance sometimes involves the search for ways in which the organisation can finesse local regulations, building relationships with host regulatory agents, for example, that enable more favourable interpretations to be secured when local employment system rules seem inconsistent with the corporate priorities expressed in corporate reward policy.

Depending on the degree of perceived dominance of the local contextual conditions, reward management practices may reflect a *preferred approach* within the matrix illustrated in Table 1, with a *fallback position* if the initial tactic fails.

Institutional drivers and reward strategy

CIPD international reward and recognition survey respondents were asked not only about the ideas influencing their reward strategy design objectives. We also asked for comment indicating the degree of perceived *structural* influences on reward strategy both internal and external to the organisation – for example, the corporate board of directors, customers, shareholders, trade unions. The aim was to assess the considerations behind expressed preferences towards more corporate or locally textured multinational reward strategy design approaches, or some opportunistically adopted halfway house.

Shareholders

Given the emphasis in corporate statements, and regular acknowledgement in the literature that commercial organisations were targeted by their corporate leaders to maximise shareholder value (and in the case of not-for-profit institutions, to ensure maximum cost-effectiveness in operational outcomes), it might have been anticipated that investors would be rated as major sources of influence on policy, including reward management.

When asked to declare the primary aim of their organisation, 80% of respondents selected 'shareholder wealth maximisation'. But when asked about the external sources of influence on their reward management policies, almost 42% of respondents claim

that shareholders have no influence at all. Around 20% perceive shareholders as influencing reward strategy to a great extent or a very great extent, the balance falling somewhere in between. (The figures at the extremes were 33.9% and 12.9% in the case of 'other corporate investors'.)

> '...when asked about the external sources of influence on their reward management policies, almost 42% of respondents claim that shareholders have no influence at all.'

Customers

In a world dominated by concern to secure competitive advantage, it is no surprise that a little over 92% of respondents said their organisation's primary aim was to enjoy 'a great representation among customers'. But about 50% went on to say that major clients or customers had affected reward strategy 'not at all' (25.8%), or only 'to a limited extent' (24.2%). Around 40% of respondents did attribute a moderate (25.8%) or large (21.0%) influence to those whose choices would either secure or deny the organisations their aspirations towards product/service market leadership.

Top management and trade unions

A perception of top management in the form of the corporate board of directors as occupying the driving seat fell just short of 50% of respondents (49.2%), although almost a quarter (23.8%) perceived the board as having little or no influence over the alignment of corporate and reward strategies. See Figure 3, opposite.

In line with prevailing wisdom concerning the decline in trade union status, 34% of respondents claim 'no influence' on the part of trade unions. Trade unions are, however, perceived as influencing reward strategy 'to a moderate extent', according to 32.2% of respondents, 11.3% of respondents arguing that unions influence reward strategy 'to a large extent'.

When we looked further at this with corporate interviewees, they felt that trade union influence still had to be factored in, especially in developing countries, and that while attempting to develop a common approach to the overall employee experience of working for a multinational, pay determination was not an area corporate policy-makers felt able to engage with to any level of detail after all. The strategic potential for standardisation perceived by Vernon (2006) could be limited to managerial workforce segments.

Responses to competitive economic conditions

The need to react to practice among multinational competitors was perceived as having a 'moderate' (37.7%) or 'large' (24.6%) or 'very large' (16.4%) impact on reward strategy (see Figure 4, opposite). Other organisations are ranked among the top three sources of ideas influencing the design and administration of the reward system. (Trade unions were included in the top three by 12.7% of respondents.)

Figure 3 ❖ **Perceived influence of corporate leadership on international reward**

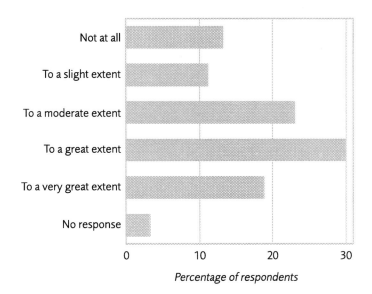

Percentage of respondents

Prevailing economic conditions are rated as outweighing political considerations: 28.6% of respondents list 'state regulations' among the top three influences on reward design and administration, while 27.9% of respondents perceive economic conditions as having 'a moderate impact', 42.6% 'a large impact', and 18% 'a very large impact'.

Skills shortages are rated as significant: 41.2% accorded them a 'great' or 'very great' influence, a further 36.5% saying a 'moderate' influence. That position notwithstanding, 19% of respondents attribute only a slight or no influence to skills

shortages. Interestingly, more than half of respondents (54%) downplay the impact of technology on international reward strategy determination, while 19% rate its influence highly. A little under a quarter (23.8%) regard the impact of technology as 'moderate'.

In summary, the adoption of a more global approach among multinationals may be perceived at the strategic level, setting reward *principles* for application to employees throughout business operations. But, as one leading management consultant interviewed for the report observed, the focus becomes

Figure 4 ❖ **Perceived impact of economic conditions on international reward**

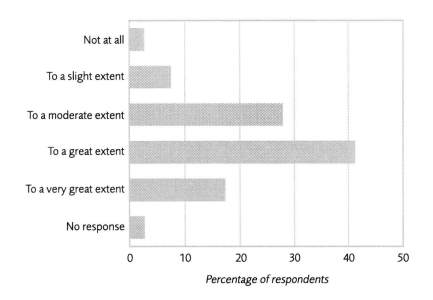

Percentage of respondents

operational at executive level. In order to support the objective of managing executives as a global talent pool, plans focus on managing the executive-level employment relationship that must be in place and controlled centrally. For example, the chief executive level (1–2% of the organisation) is nowadays more of a 'corporate resource' than an operating business resource.

Below executive level, while reward strategy design drivers may be global, operational practice remains locally rooted. In relation to the wider reward management policy, organisations are adopting a review and comment role at the centre. Some organisations have started using a sort of idealised checklist of operational factors (for example, appropriate role benchmarking to support salary administration, pay bill budgeting, appraisal systems, and so on) that operating business units should be working to. While accepting that it may not be meeting all aspects, this tool nevertheless gives the corporate centre a basis to frame the operational application of policy globally. Operating units are expected to manage the process, guided by and held accountable to the corporate standards in that overall framework. Although the full extent of this approach remains open to verification, people are being taken to task more. For example, a senior corporate executive might refuse to sign off on a particular consequence of reward management practice unless the local operation can supply evidence to support it. In other words, a more robust review process is now needed. As a result, actions to raise the operational capability levels of HR people in the businesses are reported.

Factoring in managerial and employee views

The perception of the influence of the corporate board of directors on reward strategy has already been reported. And managers' experience is ranked by 46% of respondents as among the top three influences on corporate reward management. However, in terms of intelligence to assess detailed managerial views on the reward system across the organisation internationally, fewer than half of respondents say they have in place formalised mechanisms for gathering information. A quarter claim to survey regularly (23.8%), and a further 19% say they sometimes survey formally. But more than 40% of respondents (41.3%) claim to rely on day-to-day interaction to gather such views, while 15.9% say their organisation has 'no clear processes' for assessing managerial views on the reward system.

Turning to employee opinion on the reward system internationally, 38.1% of respondents claim to survey regularly, a further 28.6% 'sometimes' surveying and 4.8% using 'briefings' and 'focus group' approaches or, again, simply 'day-to-day interaction'. More than a quarter of respondents (28.6%) say that they never survey employee opinion on the reward system.

> 'Three-quarters of respondents claimed that intelligence on employee views on the reward system is an influence on policy-making.'

Three-quarters of respondents claimed that intelligence on employee views on the reward system is an influence on policy-

making (22.2% describe it as 'critical' and 54% 'of some interest'). In the case of 12.7% of respondents, treatment of employee views depends on who is being asked among employee segments, while a further 1% finds the utility of an employee perspective is 'limited' (9.5%) or' largely irrelevant' (1.6%) to policy-making.

Managing reward design tensions in a not-for-profit agency

When organisational complexity and the demands for skills in short supply meet a conviction-centred organisation with a charity mission, choices about the balance between corporate alignment logic and national culture logic in reward strategy design require a sensitive touch. 'Pragmatic experimentalism' may be anticipated, as the following case study illustrates.

HelpAge International is a not-for-profit agency that operates a large and heterogeneous network of projects and people around the world, mainly in countries undergoing development (for example, on the African continent) and transformation (for example, eastern Europe). Its mission is to facilitate quality-of-life improvements for economically disadvantaged elderly people. To that end, sometimes HelpAge International has to mobilise teams to enter a country at short notice to help tackle an emergency – for example, the 2004 Indian Ocean tsunami.

Given the nature and scale of the organisation, highly skilled people are required, able to handle many different activities and to work at the highest standards in doing so. The market for such human capability is highly competitive. However, as a registered charity, the guiding principles associated with the employment and reward of work team members are consistency and fairness within and across the organisation. The position is complicated by the duty the organisation has to be accountable in financial terms to donors with their own opinions on appropriate pay arrangements and costs.

According to the HR director, the organisation tries to be participative and not over-centralised, but strategy design for employing and rewarding organisation members is undertaken by a small secretariat based in the London head office. Policy is applied in the 12–14 regional offices located mainly in developing countries. Currently, efforts are being made to improve the intelligence used to benchmark employee reward levels at the subset of 'development sector' organisations. While basic salary plus benefits has predominated, recently HelpAge International has experimented with offering modest levels of pay for performance to differentiate between employee contribution levels. But this has been a source of controversy. Some senior-level HelpAge International members object to this development because it does not sit well with the charity's culture and managerial style.

The following comparison of agency and resource-based approaches may help interpret the dilemma faced by HelpAge International.

> 'The market for...human capability is highly competitive.'

Strategy and workforce assumptions influencing reward design choices

Considerations underpinning reward strategy may explicitly or implicitly draw on a variety of ways of thinking about organisation and the people employed to serve the corporate purpose. It is helpful for practitioners to reflect systematically on the objectives driving reward that emerge not only as a result of external forces but also based on management's working interpretations of how these influences feed into how they should approach their corporate governance role.

Principals, agents, and transaction costs

Shareholders and investment fund managers, boards of trustees and elected or appointed representatives in public agencies may regard management's role as achieving corporate goals while minimising the cost of the range of economic transactions involved (Williamson, 1975). Accompanying such views may be an assumption that managers and other employees will need an economic incentive to be persuaded to focus on the principals' interests rather than their own. Principals may require elaborate arrangements to monitor agents' performance and to maximise transparency in reporting (Jensen and Meckling, 1976).

Key resource bundles

A different perspective on the nature of strategy and the role of management argues that *sustainable* competitiveness depends on recognising the way distinctive organisations may emerge when resources – people and the routines they engage in to produce outcomes, for example – are nurtured as bundles. These bundled resources may be perceived as organisationally valuable as well as rare. As the outcome of a unique set of experiences and interactions, distinctive resource bundles are not easy for competitors to imitate or to substitute alternative resources to create the same effect (Barney et al, 2001).

Institutionalised relationships

Complementing the resource-based view is a perspective that contends that the role of well-established relationships will count most in attempts to build sustainable organisational effectiveness. In contrast to the agency perspective, institutionally-inclined strategy reasons that groups of people in organisations will conclude that individual aims are more effectively achieved by co-ordinated action. Through shared experience of problem-solving, even when the conditions alter, lessons learned may be reproduced. So management becomes an activity more effectively concerned with creating the conditions in which people will be inclined to co-operate and work in self-directed ways that capitalise on learned benefits over time (North, 1990).

ORGANISATION STRUCTURE DRIVERS OF TRANSNATIONAL REWARD DESIGN

While practitioners may usefully reflect on these considerations, Kessler (2005) cautions against attempts to classify organisations by strategy, let alone to match reward systems leading to improved organisational effectiveness. The structure of the multinational, and the criteria governing managerial practices that logically follow, is a further area that gives rise to questions when considering international reward strategy design. Perkins and Hendry (1999a, 2001) developed the matrix in Table 2 on page 16, building on the work of Ghoshal and Bartlett (1998) to inform thinking in that context.

While not intended to be used prescriptively, examining the characteristics of current and intended organisation structure will assist multinational reward strategy designers weigh the contingencies between operational priorities, and how these are resourced, the way knowledge is generated and mobilised, and the likely interaction with the principles underlying employee effort–reward management approaches. Analysis can be cross-referenced to the managerial style categories in Table 1.

The decentralised federation

The decentralised federation represents the classic multinational organisation. This type of formation, historically popular with European businesses seeking to extend operations beyond their national borders, exhibits a control ethic largely based on the management of subsidiaries as a kind of offshore portfolio:

❖ Each national unit is managed as a separate entity focused on optimising its situation in the local environment.

❖ Reward policy tends to mirror this fragmentation: local market rates set the structure of compensation and performance recognition, and incentive plans are linked to the outcomes achieved by the quasi-independent business units. International revenues are perceived as being of limited relevance to the health of the principal entity at home.

❖ Central initiatives are taken only in instances where the local entities believe it will be to their advantage to permit them, or where the capability simply does not exist in an efficient or effective form.

❖ A trusted headquarters or parent country national (PCN) tends to be seconded on long-term expatriate conditions to oversee the employees. Provided the individual does no harm to the interests of the real business in the domestic market, that manager may become largely disconnected from corporate succession planning and related activity. A reward management **conformer–adapter** orientation appears likely.

Table 2	Multinational organisation, managerial processes and reward contingencies

Operational Focus

Decentralised federation	Local identification/exploitation of discrete opportunities
Co-ordinated federation	Deployment of 'parent' strategic competence with local adaptation
Centralised hub	Corporate headquarters strategy application to standard template
Synthesised network	Exploitation of diverse but interdependent perspectives and networked capability

Resource Focus

Decentralised federation	Local self-sufficiency – PCN[a] oversight
Co-ordinated federation	PCN core apability sourced centrally – application dispersed
Centralised hub	Centralised and globally scaled PCN dominant
Synthesised network	Multiple and flexible co-ordination of PCN, HCN[b] and TCN[c] workforce

Knowledge Management Focus

Decentralised federation	Locally emergent/retained learning
Co-ordinated federation	Centralised innovation and core learning transferred to overseas units
Centralised hub	Centrally developed/retained learning
Synthesised network	Shared corporate vision honed through multidirectional knowledge interactions

Reward Structures and Processes

Decentralised federation	Minimal consistency of approach; benchmarking to local labour markets; performance rewards based on value created in discrete markets, share of which is returned to core investor at discretion of PCN overseers at local level
Co-ordinated federation	Blueprint reward structure and systems, transfused by roving parent company agents at top levels. Disconnect between parent and local reward practice and performance objectives and recognition, other than for piecemeal 'initiatives'
Centralised hub	Discrepancies of treatment between expatriate 'headquarters' employees and locals, both in levels and delivery of reward. Emphasis on maximising return to centre from operational 'franchises'
Synthesised network	Respect for diverse traditions and local market regulation, but common framework for reward and performance, placing emphasis on shared value creation and integrative dispersion among stakeholders

Source: (based on) Perkins and Hendry (1999a, 1999b, 2001), with acknowledgement to Ghoshal and Bartlett (1998)
Notes: a. Parent Country National
         b. Host Country National
         c. Third-country National

The co-ordinated federation

The spread of US influence around the globe following the Second World War resulted in an alternative organisational model which places more influence at the centre. The co-ordinated federation reflects the fact that, in a departure from European tradition, business in the United States has tended towards large-scale operations, especially those striking out beyond domestic boundaries, run predominantly by 'professional managers' (rather than owner-managers).

> '...business in the United States has tended towards large-scale operations, especially those striking out beyond domestic boundaries, run predominantly by "professional managers".'

❖ The control ethic favours sophisticated (financial) management systems, enabling significant delegation while maintaining overall corporate control within the 'home' market institution.

❖ A unitary way of doing business, based exclusively on the parent company's domestic approach and sense of moral superiority tends to prevail under this model. The assumption is that all new ideas and development emerge from the core business located in the country of origin, although – subject to compliance with basic financial and managerial norms – local management may be permitted scope to adapt operational practices to accommodate local product market tastes and circumstances.

❖ In reward management terms, an **exporter–avoider** orientation style arises. Co-ordinated federations' culture of dependency has meant clear distinctions in reward and recognition structures and systems between the value placed on professionals and managers recruited locally (host country nationals) and parent country nationals deployed on short- to medium-term expatriate assignments to transfer the requisite knowhow, and to ensure compliance with corporate norms. Encouragement for capability development and alignment of interests, supported by appropriate reward systems, is limited.

❖ Emphasis is placed on preserving expatriates' home standards, with company-provided (or at least company-funded) residential and attendant family facilities, security and clubs, to enable the expatriate community to maintain a home-abroad community lifestyle (creating divisions, especially where superior expatriate living is funded beyond that available to home country nationals on local/national incomes). Generous hardship and incentive premiums have traditionally completed a package of secondment terms to induce the expatriate temporarily to interrupt career and personal life while abroad. Competitive challenges in the past ten years or so have raised questions regarding the ongoing credibility of maintaining this kind of expatriate compensation regime.

The centralised hub

Research suggests that commercial markets in the twentieth century tended to be dominated by a 'global triad', comprising Europe, the United States and Japan (Rugman, 2000). Ghoshal and Bartlett's (1998) 'centralised hub' configuration has been perceived as particularly suited to the managerial norms and practices of Japanese firms.

The managerial focus tends to be more on global markets overall than their counterparts in either of the 'federated' structures.

❖ The 'hub' model depends on centralised decision-making, consistent with cultures where group-oriented behaviour may translate into management systems (Hofstede, 2003). But such characteristics, depending on a complex system of personalised commitments and interdependencies, are notoriously difficult to transfer abroad.

❖ Parent country national managers transferred overseas have been found to form only a limited appreciation of local environmental differences against which commercial opportunities may be evaluated and exploited.

❖ Careers and associated reward structures remain firmly embedded in the parent company, making almost clinical distinctions in some cases between 'corporate' and other employees. An **exporter–resister** reward management style arises. Arguably, this is exemplified by Japanese companies' entry to European markets, using the employment system flexibility found in the UK as a 'bridge' for regional production centres, rather than diverting managerial energies into overt resistance towards more institutional rigidities perceived among continental European employment systems, or considering adaptation of operational templates developed at the hub for export to satellite firms.

The synthesised network

Ghoshal and Bartlett (1998) prescribe a 'transnational' solution to the competitive challenge of organising and managing across geographical borders. The synthesised network organisation benchmark directly addresses the need to develop multidimensional strategic capabilities for generating and mobilising knowledge in pursuit of competitive advantage.

> 'The synthesised network organisation benchmark directly addresses the need to develop multidimensional strategic capabilities for generating and mobilising knowledge...'

❖ The transnational, in this context, directs attention towards efficiency related to global competitiveness, and rewards and recognises appropriate behavioural inputs and performance outcomes accordingly, irrespective of whether the source is parent country nationals, home country nationals or, increasingly influential, third-country nationals, who may possess the cosmopolitan characteristics desired to support international business expansion without the cultural and financial expectations that parent country nationals traditionally carry with them. Each member of the organisation, wherever he or she may be physically (or hierarchically), forms part of the corporate learning and performance management network.

❖ The contribution of transnational employee resources may be recognised using reward programmes devised and enacted aligning corporate governance aims and continuous innovation with responsiveness to diverse market conditions.

❖ Insider knowhow and customer-responsive flexibility is combined with fleet-footedness in diffusing learning and successful practice across international operations. A **conformer–avoider–globaliser** hybrid orientation follows.

A FRAMEWORK TO BE USED CRITICALLY

Ghoshal and Bartlett's (1998) ideal type of organisational forms and contingent managerial styles and practices may be a useful basis for auditing current practice and evaluating possible strategic initiatives. However, there is evidence to suggest that the descriptions summarised in Table 2 and examined above should not be used uncritically by practitioners. Account must be taken of the way multinationals transfer practices originating in foreign subsidiaries across borders, including the reverse diffusion of employment practices (Edwards et al, 2005).

Particular problems are identified, for example, regarding the openness of US multinationals to the flow of management practice – not only outward from the parent, but in forms of networked and reverse transfer of good practice learned through experimentation and experience across foreign subsidiaries. This is in spite of the anticipation that, having been forged in the crucible of the American liberal market economy (Hall and Soskice, 2001), US companies are less constrained by regulation and more disposed to make radical changes (compared with the more co-ordinated market economy found in, say, mainland Europe or Japan). In fact, the reverse may apply.

If we follow this logic, successful international business organisation may lie in transferring ideas and other resources to a variety of differing business contexts and then empowering subsidiary managements to experiment by adapting organisational routines to local business settings. But the process does not stop there. The *learning* from this experimentation is reabsorbed and redeployed corporately. This is the rationale for the transnational solution prescribed by Ghoshal and Bartlett. But social and political influences may undermine this logic (Whitley, 2001). It may be misguided to conceive of multinationals as though they were cohesive rational actors maximising the use of resources across national boundaries. Morgan (2001) argues that the multinational must be perceived as a complex social arena within which competing groups draw on resources from their own socially embedded locations in pursuit of goals that involve interrelation and interaction with other social and economic actors.

> '...the scope for managerial innovation in employment and reward management may be less flexible...than we generally imagine.'

Pursuing the comparison between US and other multinationals further, a reported tendency towards the centrally co-ordinated federal structure suggests that US companies have a tendency to devolve considerable operational responsibility to foreign subsidiaries. But sociopolitical baggage from the country of origin may be difficult for American corporate managements to shed. More co-ordinated systems for management–employee relations, such as those found in countries like Germany and Sweden, may facilitate transformational change through management–labour coalition-building, rather than more evolutionary piecemeal variations to practice. The argument is not that barriers to diffusion of managerial best practice across multinational networks will be easy for organisations originating in co-ordinated market economies. It is just that the scope for managerial innovation in employment and reward management may be less flexible in organisations headquartered in liberal market economies than we generally imagine.

Implications of strategy and structure ideas and practice for international reward

This analysis may be extended to help understand managerial initiatives around the employee effort–reward nexus that features in multinational practice:

❖ The welfare capitalism tradition among some prominent US companies – particularly in the high-technology sector – involves keeping ahead in employee compensation terms, so as to keep the unions out. Meanwhile, in the north-east and Midwest United States, in the New Deal legacy firms, unions remain strong and relations between unions and management adversarial. The result is that attempts to

innovate in reward management are likely to prove problematic.

❖ In co-ordinated market economies, institutional arrangements to support partnership working with representatives of the workforce may leave the organisation more open to experimentation and change through pluralistic consultative arrangements.

❖ US companies tend to change their strategy more frequently in reaction to shifts from founder-family ownership to more stock-market-based forms of ownership, and tend to react to short-term downturns in revenues by cutting jobs and employment budgets.

❖ Co-ordinated market-economy-based firms tend to take a longer-term approach. This enables more fundamental changes to reward and other people management practices to be developed in an evolutionary way over time – even if the change outcome is quite transformational.

❖ US multinationals' tendency towards management centralisation may inhibit local management scope to innovate. Large numbers of central HR staff may also pursue political strategies to limit the scope for practice innovation (and reverse diffusion) among local managements. The corporate HR team may feel threatened by local initiatives that are presented as facilitating corporate learning, seeing it as the prerogative of central management to set the international policy and practice agenda. The Hewlett-Packard case study in Chapter 1, which tells of the rationalisation of the 'HP-way' (page 6), can be viewed in this light.

❖ A tendency towards regionalisation (rather than devolution to local subsidiary managements) is reported by Edwards et al (2005). This is where regional management teams are given scope to operate, provided that it is within the strictly controlled financial targets/monitoring set corporately in response to the shareholder value preoccupation. Regional space may restrict local experimentation on the detail of HR and reward management. Regional managements look to corporate specialists to set the tone and pace for reward practices to be followed by local administrators, reinforcing the centralisation of the corporate employment system overall.

> '...to accommodate socially embedded types of business and employment systems...it [may be] necessary for corporate managements to give pre-eminence to person-centred management over...profit-centred goals.

Focus on people while aiming at performance

One approach to the problem of balancing global and local tensions is to focus on people while aiming at performance (Elvira and Davila, 2005a). The argument is informed by social contract theories which direct attention specifically to multiple organisational stakeholders or partners in the employment relationship. The line of reasoning is that to accommodate socially embedded types of business and employment systems around the world, it is necessary for corporate managements to give pre-eminence to person-centred management over merely profit-centred goals.

Economic globalisation can imply convergence in the criteria against which legitimate organisation is evaluated. However, adopting a less deterministic stance, the influence of dominant Anglo-American corporate governance norms and ideologies infused, for example, through Westernised education and related experience remain subject to *interpretation* by those in managerial roles across different countries based on their initial local socialisation and allegiances. The hybrid managerial regime emerging from examination of CIPD international reward survey respondents' views may be a reflection of such developments. Experiential learning from a trial-and-error orientation may be transfused across the multinational network, creating distinctive capability at the transnational level for competitive advantage.

While not making claims towards generalisation, practice reported in two case study organisations (BG and Unilever) investigated as part of the research for this report may help to stimulate reflection on the ways in which multinational managements may attempt to resolve the strategy tensions we have been considering. Differences not only in terms of product market but also in the character of the businesses and managerial traditions imply that decision-makers reject simply transplanting generalised performance and reward management prescriptions to support knowledge mobilisation. Instead, they may find value in refining both formal and informal processes to meet their particular circumstances and managerial preferences.

A focus on accountability

To limit possible barriers to the networking of knowledge between **Unilever**'s branded lines of business and geographical regions, to support corporate priorities, a new group chief executive has taken a lead in stressing the importance of accountability in 'One Unilever'. Initiatives have been launched to address unnecessary complexity and intellectualism that risks inefficiencies through duplication of effort across business operations (for example, in managing product development or marketing activity).

Following definition of what corporate management wants the organisation to do, action has been taken in the case of senior managers to state explicitly where everyone's role starts and ends, with examples of what good performance looks like. Clarifying accountability across corporate networks, on the one hand, is expected to reduce misalignment with corporate policy and cost-effective mobilisation of skill sets. On the other hand, there is an attempt to make people management more than reading off detailed rules from functionally-policed

templates. In reward management terms, detailed decisions about policy application in individual cases are being devolved to line managers to increase transparency. This is perceived as a culture change accompanying the new accountability, requiring local managerial judgement within the performance-oriented corporate principles.

> *Managers are no longer asked to just fill in a spreadsheet box that in corporate HR we change the numbers for afterwards anyway.*

Scale and performance management

In approaching reward strategy design, an important contingency is scale of operations – but it is important to be clear about what scale implies in these circumstances. Complexity in achieving transparent performance-aligned accountability, and the culture change perceptions surrounding greater delegation to managers in making substantive decisions about reward outcomes, can be perceived as a function of the organisational processes associated with employing large numbers of people around the world.

BG's focus is on understanding, building and supplying natural gas markets. The group company currently has operations in 20 countries over five continents. Although headquartered in the UK, more than 60% of the workforce is based in other countries. A relative newcomer to the global energy market – but, at £15 billion, already valued beyond a company such as Unilever in market capital terms – BG's management takes it for granted that *interpersonal* interaction will underpin performance management practice. Rather than consistency review procedures, outcomes are governed by significant amounts of managerial dialogue when reaching individual pay progression decisions. With fewer than 5,000 people employed directly across worldwide operations, the global reward architect's perception is that it is much easier to communicate the agreed strategy – all the dimensions of it – through the course of the year: 'You know where you are and what you're on.' When salary increases or bonuses for managers are under consideration, the exercise is handled on the basis of discussions among people rather than following formalised performance management mechanisms.

> *Each of the managing directors says why somebody has done very well, or why somebody has done average, why somebody is poor.*

While multinational managements may be able to take advantage of size to avoid slavishly following best practice that appears to require structuring pay management in an overly formalised way, there is also a downside, as acknowledged in BG – for example:

> *The downside is that, if you're a newcomer to the organisation, it's an organisation that's been there*

for a very short period of time. You find that people who have been in the company have a much better understanding of who is a good performer and who is not a good performer.

However, BG management regards itself as fairly ruthless in tackling poor performance. The company sets very aggressive externally benchmarked targets which are communicated externally, with logical consequences for shareholder expectations.

Having done that, if the Group doesn't deliver, it will pay a very, very dear price. So ... it's not so much the process of performance management as the transparent way in which the performance assessment is done. In one respect, it's a high-risk strategy. But in another respect it shows you really go after it.

ACTION POINTERS IN INTERNATIONAL REWARD STRATEGY DESIGN

In approaching international reward strategy design, based on the express preoccupations among multinational managements, as discussed in Chapter 1, attention may be focused on two overarching aims:

- to acquire and network skills sets as the medium through which to mobilise diverse human capital, aligned with corporate purpose, on terms that are cost-effective

- to build legitimacy across all international employee categories regarding consistency in effort–reward calibration in order to sustain the integrity of the system, based on shared experiences and learning, and to retain an international resource bundle that is valuable, rare, inimitable and not substitutable.

> 'Preferred managerial style, the extent to which the multinational is structured in...synthesised terms, and the degree of opportunism when interpreting space for corporate action...all play a part in influencing international reward design choices.

We can see traces of each of the four organisational strategy perspectives summarised earlier, challenging international reward

architects to reconcile discernible tensions in the reward management structures and processes that follow. Preferred managerial style, the extent to which the multinational is structured in more or less synthesised terms, and the degree of opportunism when interpreting space for corporate action in specific contexts, all play a part in influencing international reward design choices.

Objectives for international reward management

Picking up Duncan Brown's (2001) challenge with which we opened this part of the report, and in turn building on commentary by Briscoe and Schuler (2004), three operational objectives for designing international reward and recognition systems may be distilled from the above two global strategic aims:

- Design reward systems that establish and maintain internal comparability in recognising the interdependency of employees across the multinational, whether mobilised internationally or as members of local workforces employed around the world, relating effort–reward as perceived by management and employees alike as consistent and reasonable. In this way, employees with the skills perceived by corporate management as necessary to mobilise corporate knowledge and operating routines will be attracted and retained on terms that encourage positive relations between PCNs, HCNs and TCNs to realise corporate strategy across international operations.

- Facilitate transfers between the strategic nodes on the multinational organisation network – including intersubsidiary transfers, transfers from overseas subsidiaries to locations within the parent organisation (usually headquarters), and transfers from the parent organisation and locations beyond assignees' country of origin.

- Maintain reward levels and associated practices that may be judged reasonable in relation to practices exercised by competitors in employment systems (an 'external comparability' factor), while limiting non-productive costs associated with employment as far as possible.

Bearing in mind the definitions of the employee effort–reward nexus discussed in Chapter 1, and the implications for managerial action, these aims and objectives may be refined by reflection on the nature and assumptions underlying corporate strategic priorities outlined above. The exercise will also bring to light the tensions between the aspects listed and organisational contexts, and will improve understanding of opportunities and limitations and the implications of making alternative policy choices. Operational considerations around managing international reward follow in Chapter 3.

MANAGING INTERNATIONAL REWARD AND RECOGNITION PROCESSES

3

❖ **Published evidence on reward management practices across regions.**

❖ **Practitioner views on managing international reward.**

❖ **Trends in managing expatriate compensation.**

❖ **Performance management and IT-enabled standardisation initiatives.**

The working assumption informing this research report is that multinational managements' general aim is to secure and deploy the skills to generate and mobilise knowledge to build sustainable value and sustainable competitive advantage. This ambition means that corporate managements might need to concern themselves more than they traditionally have with the detail of how the employment relationship is organised at all workforce levels, leading to the adoption of more standardised practices. The focus of attention now shifts from design to operation.

We begin by surveying the field of what has recently been published on rewarding and recognising employees across a variety of regions worldwide. Then we turn to the empirical evidence that informs this report to help address two key operational questions:

❖ What is happening to reward systems associated with international employee mobility?

❖ How are the evolving managerial issues that have a bearing on multinational effort–reward determination being generally interpreted in multinationals?

In each case, *how technology is used* emerges as an interesting phenomenon associated with organisational goals to achieve, on the one hand, accountability and performance enhancements and, on the other, standardisation and simplification.

MANAGING REWARD IN DIFFERENT REGIONS

A transregional perspective is adopted here to help us consider the possible effects on the *application* of 'global' reward strategies in different parts of the world. Given space considerations, many nuances applicable at the level of individual country will be lost in this review, but the intention is not to be encyclopaedic. The purpose is to raise issues focusing more detailed reflection shaping managerial initiatives associated with strategy application.

As in Chapter 2, the evidence suggests experimentation in financial reward management practice, indicative of emergent strategy, rather than attempts to read off a common template. Differences are perceptible between reports of what employers say they are doing and the findings of organisational research on practice outcomes in different regions of the world. An ongoing managerial priority seems to be to reduce the guarantees surrounding employment that at least a favoured few across the various employment systems enjoyed for several decades during the mid-twentieth century.

Europe

The Federation of European Employers reported in March 2005 that for most European employees living standards are gradually being harmonised and skill differentials are changing. Now market value rather than state regulation or collective bargaining takes a more central role in wage determination. But a huge divide remains between long-term EU member countries such as France and Germany, and the emergent accession states such as Poland and Hungary. As an example of the narrowing pay gap, in 2001 hourly pay in Denmark was 39 times greater than in Romania, but by the beginning of February 2005 the gap had narrowed to 22 times. The reason for this is that between 2001 and 2005 hourly pay in Denmark rose by only 18%, whereas in Romania it rose by 115% (FedEE, 2005).

> '...a huge divide remains between long-term EU member countries such as France and Germany, and the emergent accession states such as Poland and Hungary.'

Other headline issues include:

- a narrowing of relative pay levels across European countries generally. Reasons include the emergence of a more coherent labour market across the EU countries as people increasingly move to work in other countries and it becomes easier to live in one country and work in another

- a struggle among western European countries to restrain labour costs in the face of competition from eastern Europe, India and the Far East

- poorer countries experiencing inward foreign direct investment (FDI) and governments in countries such as Belarus and Moldova increasing salary levels to stave off social unrest

- a decline in collective pay bargaining as employment system liberalisation extends its influence along with the Anglo-Saxon multinational vehicles for FDI.

Knowledge mobilisation and expatriation

Knowledge mobilisation mediated through people mobilisation continues to exercise management in European multinationals. The 2005 survey conducted on behalf of the World Federation of Personnel Management Associations (WFPMA) found, looking three years into the future, that European HR specialists perceive the international mobility of employees as problematic (27% of respondents). Other top three concerns are change management (29%) and organisational effectiveness (39%). So it is no surprise to find European organisations reviewing their policies on rewarding expatriates – Shell, for example, has been conducting a back-to-basics assessment of what employee mobility means for the organisation and the consequences for the terms on offer to mobilise large numbers of people at all times to support core business activities.

Directional convergence, not final convergence

It has been argued that there is an accepted hierarchy between economies, the current dominant society setting a good practice benchmark from which others are encouraged to borrow (Smith and Meiksins, 1995, cited by Tregaskis and Brewster, 2006). But the signs of marketisation and integration across Europe should not be read as complete convergence – especially not as simple conformance to reward management norms imported from the United States. While noting directional convergence (similarity in trends), 'final convergence' (similarity in practices) is far from inevitable, argue Tregaskis and Brewster (2006).

Intraregional competition between, for example, prevailing work organisation models (and employee reward strategy) implies that the outcome may be continued diversity in the context for managerial practice between countries. Europe offers a particularly interesting setting to explore the dynamics of convergence and divergence. In practice, benchmarking pressures, locating economic market forces ahead of political factors, interface with regulatory forces derived from attempts to constitute a continent-wide set of institutions. These, in turn, are confronted by a variety of national practices that sit in tension with

transnational initiatives to set minimum standards, for example, related to employment protection and working time across the EU (see the box below for a comparative example).

> ### Internal versus external labour market practice
>
> Ideas associated with Anglo-American forms of corporate governance that encourage corporate managers to rely on external economic markets to determine the price of labour may be particularly at odds with a tendency in **Germany** to acknowledge the economic viability of maintaining internal labour markets and strong wage levels. German works councils are recognised as playing a key role in the reproduction of this employment system. These ideas set the context for managerial choices, legitimised by reference to the emphasis on a quality-based production regime that relies on a highly skilled workforce developed through an elaborate apprenticeship system, underwritten by a major financial commitment by organisations to develop firm-specific skills. Reliance on external markets to regulate employment and reward levels is perceived as less attractive when key skills are not easily transferable across organisations. Again, opportunistic behaviour among multinationals may be anticipated.
>
> Contrasting with the German example, in **Spain** employers are increasingly attracted to practices intended to weaken traditional rigidities in the employment system, enabled by the incidence of high unemployment levels and legislative reforms. Trade unions have traditionally played a powerful role in the employment system, and skills development practices have militated against interorganisational transferability. However, prevailing economic conditions and the vulnerability of certain groups of either underqualified or overqualified workers for the employment opportunities currently available have encouraged perceptions among employers of the economic viability of shifting to more external employment market regulation.

Tregaskis and Brewster (2006) use a dataset enabling comparisons to be made across a sample of European countries over a ten-year period. They find some convergence indications in terms of increased flexibility in employment practices to support the corporate governance aims pursued by multinational managements. However, final convergence appears uncertain in the light of apparent differences in organisational practice originally measured across countries in the early 1990s and still in evidence a decade later.

So the embeddedness of certain practices has to be taken into account when multinational managements encounter pressures to adopt best practices either from global or pan-European sources. Citing research findings by Kostova and Roth (2002), Tregaskis and Brewster (2006) conclude that multinational management practice is an indication that multinational subsidiaries engage in different patterns of practice adoption across European employment systems, depending on the favourability of the institutional context. This finding echoes the argument by Bloom *et al* (2003) and the CIPD survey findings examined in Chapter 2.

North America: from re-engineers to cost-contained organisational leaders?

In North America, reward management pressures may arise from concern among HR practitioners with leadership, substituting an emphasis in the recent past on re-engineering and restructuring. Those consulted as part of the 2005 WFPMA survey said that they wished organisation leaders would appreciate the distinction between leadership and management when attempting organisational change to accommodate problems of expansion.

> 'Those consulted as part of the 2005 WFPMA survey said that they wished organisation leaders would appreciate the distinction between leadership and management...'

North American HR specialists are also anxious about succession planning due to a wave of retirements in the coming five years. In an employment market where the emphasis is on generic rather than firm-specific skills, facilitating mobility of individuals, reward management initiatives will be required to address likely wage escalation during succession-planning talent competitions. The emphasis on rewarding contribution may be around the need to operate at less of a re-engineering manager level and more at the level of leader, co-ordinating complex people and process factors to achieve specified organisational effectiveness criteria (without the threat of job cuts to cajole workforce members into compliant behaviour).

However, governance pressures will mean attention to keeping total compensation costs under control in spite of the competitive employment market. On the direct compensation-related front, HR specialists consulted by WFPMA remain exercised by the high cost of employee benefits – to be anticipated given the demographic situation (an ageing workforce). The people–performance nexus appears set to be a site of potential tension in the future, creating difficulties not only for employers based in North America but also for multinationals that wish to draw on North American executives to resource their organisations on the opposite side of the Atlantic. As one UK-headquartered corporate specialist commented when interviewed as part of this research, referring to problems the organisation had encountered following moves to import a significant proportion of senior executives from the United States:

> *Due to regulatory considerations in the UK, there are aspects that a US recruit may take for granted, such as restricted stock without performance conditions, which would not be tolerated among UK institutional investors.*

Latin America

Two dimensions from the influential cross-cultural management framework developed by Geert Hofstede –power distance and collectivism – can be used to explore the influence of national culture in the functioning of Latin American organisations. Elvira and Davila (2005a) translate the Hofstede (2003) dimensions into what they term the value categories – respect for authority and social relationships – to form a hybrid cultural Latin American management model. This is characterised by a humanistic orientation to work and labour market institutions. Work in Latin America fulfils a worker's social as well as economic needs. Social recognition becomes an important motivator to be co-operative and loyal, important traits in a collectivistic society.

Applying this thinking to reward and recognition management, Elvira and Davila (2005a) cite research in Mexico by Diaz-Saenz and Witherspoon (2000). Family is central in Latin American workers' lives, and the researchers found that employees base their work decisions and expectations on their family needs. In general, work is seen as the means to a single and important aim: to provide a good quality of life for the employee's family. Institutional support for this cultural feature comes from labour legislation. For example, Mexican labour laws were created to promote social welfare, especially in the face of recurrent economic crises between the mid-1970s and mid-1990s. Underlying this legislation is the premise that economic crises impact on workers' salaries but not their fringe benefits, which are tax-free. The legal objective is to maintain the quality of life of workers' families.

Rewards (and recognition) carry a different cultural meaning according to employees' organisational level – executives versus blue-collar worker (Diaz-Saenz and Witherspoon, 2000, cited by Elvira and Davila, 2005a). Reward systems may become contentious when based on performance appraisals:

- The impact of performance appraisals is tinted by a work culture that avoids conflicts between superior and subordinates.

- Performance appraisals are therefore controversial by definition and their outcomes are rarely used.

- Collectivist culture means that Latin Americans tend to value social relationships manifested through personal communication and empathy among organisational members.

- Additionally, subordinates value dependence on a superior for decision-making; they shy away from responsibility.

Elvira and Davila (2005b) argue that the reliance on authority decentralisation inherent in modern management work systems clashes with the Latin American's preference for centralisation and organisational hierarchy. Multinational reward system designers should reflect on issues that may arise from attempts to devolve accountability accompanied by individualised contingent pay systems. Operational problems may be amplified by attempts to increase reliance on technology across complex transnational organisational networks, in substitution for personal contact to support efficient manager–employee performance management communications. (This is examined further below.)

Australia

Kaye (1999) argues that the people–performance nexus in Australia has been affected by system-wide managerial interventions linking HR management to strategic planning and cultural change, reinforcing the use of the hard model of HR management. While this may be a setting quite different from that specified for socially-oriented Latin cultures, a strong collectivist tradition may militate against initiatives that prioritise management aspects above human aspects when managing employment relations:

❖ Australian organisations have shown greater interest in rewarding employees to perform in line with organisational strategic goals. But putting pay at risk is not new here. The 1995 Australian Workplace and Industrial Relations Survey reported that a third of the workplaces surveyed had a performance-based pay system for their non-managerial employees.

❖ Employer initiatives have attempted explicitly to reinforce the relationship between strategy and performance, linking individual financial rewards to company performance.

❖ But while competitive business strategies may be improving the bottom line in operations located in Australia, the association between strategic HR management and greater job insecurity, especially when workers are being viewed as a commodity in a labour market, has reportedly produced lower job satisfaction.

❖ Disengagement may be counterproductive when the emphasis of multinational strategy creates knowledge-based interdependencies.

❖ As reported in the North American case, the prospect may be a search for talent capable of providing values-based 'leadership' delineated from cost-centred 'management'.

> '...if the intention behind "strategic" people management approaches is to strategise around reward determination, for example, ...HR management must be reconceptualised to acknowledge the human endeavour of organisations.'

Kaye (1999) concludes that if the intention behind 'strategic' people management approaches is to strategise around reward determination, for example, in conjunction with an organisation's business direction, HR management must be reconceptualised to acknowledge the human endeavour of organisations.

The message for practitioners is clear. What indication of managerial style do organisation leaders wish to communicate? Are people a substitutable commodity in a labour market? Or is the relationship with those through whom knowledge is to be generated and mobilised something demanding a more humanistic (rather than exclusively economic) orientation? Where do multinational managements wish to position reward policies and practices on the people–performance spectrum in arranging the balance between global standards and their local application?

China, Japan and South Korea

Rowley et al (2004) criticise the view that culture and institutions form the major stumbling-blocks to the possible decline and weakening of national employment systems and the HR management practices that follow.

Placing the focus on 'regional clusters', the researchers argue that these constraints may dissipate where geographical and cultural closeness and 'openness' to similar economic pressures exist, leading to HR management convergence. China, Japan and South Korea are presented as such a cluster and the emergence of an identifiable 'Asian' model of HR management is suggested. Reward management implications may be seen in a greater emphasis on pay for performance, as seniority-based lifetime employment norms have been challenged managerially. As with the contrast between directional and final convergence trends in Europe cited by Tregaskis and Brewster (2006), however, Rowley et al (2004) distinguish between levels of occurrence and acceptance.

China

In China there has been a shift towards performance-based rewards. Before the reforms started under the Deng administration, for a protected minority (about one in seven), worker remuneration was integrally linked with the institutional framework of the 'iron rice bowl'. Wages were predictable, based on an eight-scale Soviet template; the pace of work was steady; labour turnover was low, even rare. Reforms to employment contract management in the early 1990s introduced performance-related remuneration. Evaluation became increasingly geared to performance criteria, particularly in large enterprises, whether state-owned or outside the state sector. As part of the reforms that have promoted labour market advances in China, the system of lifetime employment was being phased out as part of a convergence package, albeit with Chinese characteristics, as the country entered the World Trade Organisation at the end of 2001.

Japan

In Japan considerable barriers to change and the desire not to destroy what was, and in many cases still is, perceived to be a highly competitive management system means that change is expected to be gradual and incremental. But the hollowing out of manufacturing, rising unemployment, the ageing of the population and the changing expectations of younger employees have meant that some change is regarded as inevitable. Employee resourcing and remuneration are singled out as the most likely areas for change. Short-term contracts and 'casualisation' of employment will continue to increase, and remuneration will be tied more and more to performance. Evaluation of employees linked to performance criteria has accompanied the reported demise of lifetime employment, seniority wages and age-based promotions. Survey research findings indicate that over 80% of companies are using ability and performance criteria in managerial promotion decisions. Multinational incursions into the Japanese employment system are instrumental in the change trend as well.

Graduates are reported as seeking the challenge of merit-based pay and promotion offered by foreign companies. Unions, while opposed to these developments in the past, have begun to accept a limited application of a merit-based system for determining pay.

South Korea

In Korea, at the macro level, a core feature of an annual wage offensive has been the establishment of guidelines for contract negotiations at individual enterprise level, albeit with less consistency at regional or craft level. The guidelines have been designed by the Federation of Korean Trade Unions with the Ministry of Labour. At the micro level, the system of seniority-based remuneration has been questioned. There have been changes – not only wage freezes and reducing bonuses and benefits, but also annual pay, with salary based on individual ability or performance, employee share options and profit-sharing. At the same time, there has been some shift in the basis of evaluation from length of service towards work performance. However, a range of practices exists between pure seniority and performance, and changes are relatively limited in coverage and spread. For instance, seniority continues to have a role in the reward systems in many firms, very few basing pay progression decisions exclusively on performance. Annual pay practices are reported as being limited to managers or the higher educated, while some firms use a base-up remuneration system, with a uniform increase of basic pay regardless of performance. For instance, Hyundai's stock option plan covers just 7% of the workforce, while Samsung's profit-sharing has been limited to researchers, although Rowley et al (2004) report that since 2000 this has been extended to all university graduates. Critically, many managers argue that while seniority should change, they do not disregard its merits entirely.

India

For about the last decade and a half, the Indian business system has been undergoing the transition from state-regulated to liberalised market economy (Budhwar and Khatri, 2001). Competition is likely to lead organisations to try to distinguish themselves in the ways they mobilise knowledge and skills through more effective people management.

> 'Competition is likely to lead organisations [in India] to try to distinguish themselves in the ways they mobilise knowledge and skills through...effective people management.'

One of the aspects that researchers have been tracking is the devolution of responsibility for HR management practices to Indian managers. In the case of pay and benefits, recent survey evidence indicates that 42% of Indian enterprises have been delegating pay and benefits management to the line, 54% devolving performance appraisal. This has been accompanied by reported investment in training in associated areas, although the need for caution in generalising from the survey evidence is stressed as the transitional period may, once again, imply a gap between aspiration and current practice.

Applying this thinking to the ways in which pay levels are determined, there is evidence to suggest a subtle transition towards more westernised norms for pay-setting. Budhwar and Khatri's (2001) survey indicates that:

❖ While a quarter of organisations determine pay based on length of service (or 'total work experience'), nearly 27% of organisations link pay with skills and competency attainment, and over 48% link pay and individual performance.

❖ In 54% of Indian organisations surveyed, pay and benefits levels are determined on the basis of some mixture of service, competencies and performance.

❖ A lag is reported in the Indian public sector compared with the private sector. The rate of change is attributed to a combination of Indian cultural values (where age is given importance) and legal requirements (Budhwar and Boyne, 2004).

Africa

Kamoche (2002) argues that multinational firms have an important role to play in African economies, being well placed to stimulate the development of human capital, not merely through the traditional routes of creating employment and diffusing knowledge through expatriates but also through African experts who have gained knowledge by working in the west.

Rather than trying to make a developing economy more like Europe and North America, multinational managements should explore the indigenous roots of approaches that are suitable for Africa. Attention is directed towards the east, as managers, particularly from some southern African countries, begin to cultivate business relations with their counterparts in east Asia. In place of a comparative focus on developed/developing convergence/divergence, elements of 'cross-vergence' should be embraced with particular regard to the diffusion of high-performance work practices.

> 'The 2005 WFPMA survey...in Africa contrasts compensation as a three-year-old problem, whereas change management is listed as a "today" and "tomorrow" issue...'

Anakwe's (2002) analysis of organisations across three major cities in Nigeria found a blend of western or foreign practices and local practices in HR management, attributed to the significance of the local context. The 2005 WFPMA survey of HR professionals in Africa contrasts compensation as a three-year-old problem (31%), whereas change management is listed as a 'today' (63%) and 'tomorrow' issue (31%), in relation to which compensation trails off to 6% in both instances. Employee rewards, more broadly defined, are, however, listed as a future issue in 13% of cases. A shift away from authoritarian management is cited in qualitative commentary as a pressing issue. As in the case of the Latin American situation, pay and other forms of employee reward may have a role to play in facilitating change and in their mode of delivery, symbolising a change in management style that blends normative westernised practice with more indigenous organisational principles.

A collectivist orientation is consistent with the principle of the traditional African system of organisation in which the responsibilities of group members are derived from the work-group activities rather than from specific jobs, and teamwork is emphasised. Blending contribution pay approaches with organisation around the work group rather than job- and person-based rewards could therefore offer a workable hybrid that retains the focus on performance while accommodating working orientations in the local context.

Opportunities for strategic reward management

This brief transregional review implies that although care is needed when attempting northern–southern hemisphere reward management transplants, common principles may be activated corporately. In summary, here are some action pointers:

❖ In North America, but also discernible generally, the significant factor is an orientation towards leadership in reward administration rather than simply anticipating convergence along westernised 'best practice' lines. A managerial style characterised by re-engineering and cost-cutting alone risks workforce disengagement, as noted in the Australian data.

❖ Opportunities exist for HR specialists to play a strategic and educational role accompanying the devolution of operational decisions to line management. In regional blocs such as East Asia, provided that – as witnessed in evidence from Europe – 'final' convergence outcomes are not taken for granted – a similar 'strategic support' role may be performed.

❖ In mature markets, an ongoing 'talent war' is expected to undermine efforts to dampen pay bill pressures, at least among core sources of knowledge and skills and their mobilisation across multinational networks, as well as the embedded norms and values impacting on interpretation by different groups of managers.

MANAGING INTERNATIONAL REWARD: VIEWS FROM PRACTITIONERS

Consistent with reward design commentary and the discussion of data recording regional practice trends, evidence from the CIPD international reward and recognition survey, complemented by a series of face-to-face discussions with reward specialists in multinationals, puts the accent on change. Particular emphasis is given to integrating organisational networks around common governance principles. And considerable attention is being focused on standardisation and simplification, as well as on ensuring consistent attention to performance accountabilities. This applies to skills acquisition and deployment involving physical mobilisation as well as mediated through reliance on indigenous talent.

We turn our attention initially to reflection on international mobility practices, followed by corporate initiatives – including the deployment of technological resources – to improve performance-aligned reward management and to enhance the consistency of reward administration practices in general.

Issues around knowledge mobilisation requiring the expatriation of people

In the words of a senior international HR adviser, 'Managing international mobility is still as difficult and as easy as it always has been.' In terms of reward management, 'What has grown up is a much easier acceptance of different ways of doing things.' This has given rise to the need for greater pragmatism in organising the terms of mobility, and requiring a shift in the role played by corporate HR specialists: 'to educate and facilitate the *management* of international mobility, not take on accountability for controlling and accounting for cost'. However, the influence of role models at the very top remains a cause for concern in some instances.

In multinationals across a variety of sectors – including Boots, BT, Cable and Wireless, Cadbury Schweppes, Citigroup, Diageo and Shell – a commonly reported concern is to reappraise the basis on which expatriation has been managed. Deliberations reflect an effort to address the tensions surrounding demands for decision-making closest to the business context while ensuring that the architecture is in place to achieve corporate consistency and governance aims. Questions are being asked about the essential purpose of deploying employees internationally when the cost levels are high. A greater variety of models of mobility are being experimented with, leading some multinational managements to revisit the basic definition of mobility. The result has been a shift away from a unitary notion of expatriation, replacing it with the idea of positioning mobility requirements within a continuum (Figure 5, opposite) – something that Shell has been reflecting on.

A spectrum of employee mobility

Beyond those who are engaged in frequent or extended travel on an international and intercontinental basis, there are so-called Monday-to-Friday workers – long-term commuters who live in one country but spend the working week based in another country that is within weekend travelling distance. Some are home-based. They spend perhaps several days in an office when travelling between different locations, and for the remainder work from their base.

Towards the other end of the range, there are the more traditional international assignments. Here, the response now tends to be 'Let's not allow the technical issues to interfere with meeting business needs.' Flexibility is seen as more important than simply policing the details of the policy. A senior European management consultant told us that the HR response is being influenced by the need 'to support business requirements, even if this means a higher cost', however these costs are managed in the business. In that context, the HR functional intervention is to explain how much it will cost to meet the business need in mobilising an individual internationally, then the business must budget for and explain this cost managerially up the line.

> *More and more companies are being pragmatic. At one stage over the past few years there was a tendency*

Figure 5   Shell's international mobility continuum

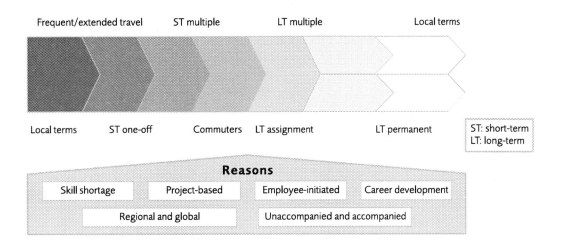

among some organisations still to require mobility on the part of individuals while 'screwing the package down'. People have learned that this was counterproductive.

Equity, experience – and potential fast-track career recognition

An angle that apparently has not been sacrificed, and that expatriation specialists have traditionally overseen, is the sense of fairness in terms of balancing what the business wants and what is fair to employees. In **Citigroup,** the principle governing international assignment terms is that the individual is there to make a difference, to help local people grow.

While the expatriate may be replaced by another one, we're finding more and more that local people are replacing the traditional style of expat, whose role was 'spreading Citi DNA' from US nationals to a diverse population now distributed across more than 100 countries.

This has led to a recalibration of international assignment packages. The intended shift in philosophy is that employees are going to be treated reasonably. Attractive rewards will be available for consistent high performance, complementing 'a rich experience and a good life'. But 'They're not going to make a [financial] killing on this sort of situation.'

And I think we're also repositioning it to say it's a kind of a win–win where you go there, you get different exposure, different experience, good fast-track, good career. Certainly if you move on, it seems you're on people's radar.

Smarter package design

Business cost pressures have concentrated corporate attention on 'getting smarter about package design'. As in the case of Shell, attention in Citigroup has been on understanding what the

purpose of the international mobility programme is. Plan types have been modified accordingly. Regional plans have been introduced, 'because it does seem absurd to pay somebody in dollars and then move them around Euroland'.

> 'Gaining top management attention may stimulate awareness among operational managers that one basis on which their performance...is being judged is aligning international employee assignment oversight with managing for value goals.'

While the main considerations probably remain cost and value, there are aspirations to strengthen processes that may facilitate greater understanding (and transparency) of the source of value from international assignments, provided the topic finds its way on to the top management agenda. Efforts by corporate specialists to inform and guide (as well as audit) operational management practice may be more effective following this transition at the level of significant detail. Gaining top management attention may stimulate awareness among operational managers that one basis on which their performance contribution to the organisation is being judged is aligning international employee assignment oversight with managing for value goals. Awareness of this kind may stimulate demand for specialist counsel, and receptiveness to educational initiatives by the HR function.

A wider stakeholder conversation

Creating the conditions for a more comprehensively informed discussion – involving a wider set of stakeholders – before assignments are initiated may help to ensure that international assignment policies are applied as intended, subjecting exceptions to greater scrutiny. The discussions reported here suggest a shift to generic international assignment policies as part of the attempt to standardise and make more transparent the application of principles governing practice. (For example, in Boots Group a new long-term assignment policy launched in March 2005 integrates at least three prior schemes into a single streamlined version.)

Reported managerial emphasis among all the multinationals studied appears to be on developing new frameworks to meet new needs (matched to geographical contexts) while eliminating personal deals. Increasing knowledge and ownership surrounding international assignment administration among line managers in the multidivisional organisation, explicitly aligned with value-based principles, appears firmly under the spotlight for attention.

PAY-FOR-PERFORMANCE STANDARDISATION ACROSS THE MULTINATIONAL WORKFORCE

This greater performance emphasis surfaces in the talk among practitioners when describing the governing principles for international reward management generally – even if action and philosophy presently are more inclined to directional rather than final convergence. When invited to comment on linking rewards and performance, although over two-thirds of respondents to the CIPD international reward and recognition survey claim to have a pay-for-performance *philosophy* applicable internationally, the number fell to well below half who applied it *in practice*. And 6.5% of respondents claimed never to link pay with appraised

performance in practice. See Table 3, below.

Where a direct link is claimed between reward and performance, almost three-quarters of respondents say this is associated with basic pay (73.8%), and 85.2% of respondents say the link is to variable bonus payments. Over a third (34.4%) of respondents report that performance appraisal is linked with non-cash recognition. In terms of the factors determining pay progression practices overall, respondents seem almost equally influenced by market benchmarking as by performance appraisal. And the figures did not differ much whether considering pay progression arrangements applicable to managerial employees or to those employed below managerial levels. See Table 4, below.

Probably representative of the kinds of claims made publicly as the purpose of reward policies is this statement:

> To attract, retain and motivate our people by providing a clear, flexible and market-competitive reward package, which reinforces the business strategy, rewards great performance and helps to make [Enterprise X] a great place to be.

On the other hand, from an employee's perspective it is acknowledged that people in general tend to view reward in terms of what it delivers to them rather than what the group hopes it will achieve, so that if someone not directly connected with corporate

Table 3 Are pay and other rewards directly linked to performance appraisal?

Percentage of respondents saying...

	Always	Sometimes	Never
In philosophy	67.7	27.4	4.8
In practice	38.7	54.8	6.5
In perception	24.2	72.6	3.2

Table 4 Pay progression determination

	Managerial employees (%)	Non-management employees (%)
Market benchmarking	63.5	60.5
Individual negotiation	22.2	3.2
Collective bargaining	3.2	20.6
Length of service	9.5	12.7
Skills/competency levels	n/a	30.2
Performance appraisal	71.4	63.5
Management discretion/other	44.4	39.6

HR was asked to comment on what the company's reward philosophy was, he or she would probably answer 'paying the market median'. In practice, the more pragmatic aspiration is to apply the corporate principles in an underpinning, not sole-driver, way. Reward is therefore a key support to those in decision-making contexts. Looking at the issue from the opposite angle, if we get it wrong, it is acknowledged that negative consequences are likely to follow. The philosophy may be used managerially, in practice, as a mirror against which each element of employee reward may be held up to see whether (and how) each element is contributing (or not) to the summative aspiration – at the effort–reward nexus, doing enough to get enough in return.

Common principles – segmented application linked to different markets

Application of the philosophy is consistent but it feels different in its application to people whose pay is linked to different markets – examples offered at the extremes contrasted group executive directors with employees in call centres. The challenge comes when people are less interested. Under these circumstances, making an organisation an exciting place to be demands more managerially than, say, extending this philosophy to people nearer the top of the managerial hierarchy. In terms of international comparisons, from observational encounters, each workforce segment seems to have more in common, regardless of location, and therefore the difference remains between the segments/ levels. One respondent described a visit to a call centre in the United States where the same issues were in evidence as those applicable among similar work groups in the UK.

Differentiating between workforce segments, the fact that 200,000 people around the world occupying what Unilever calls Level 1 positions (non-managerial employees – plantation workers, factory workers, salespeople, and so on), for example, are frequently in unionised roles is perceived as a constraint on the amount of influence on explicit reward management that can be achieved corporately, in practice.

Performance recognition in the not-for-profit sector

Explicit pay-for-performance management remains controversial, especially beyond the commercial sector. **HelpAge International** is a very diverse organisation, employing over 70 nationalities right up to senior management level. Trustees are likewise – the board is incredibly diverse: a majority of members are female and from developing countries. There is an emphasis on building up local capacity, employing people from the regions concerned, reducing a reliance on expatriates and keeping the London head office slim.

The guiding principles for reward management are consistency and fairness within and across the organisation. Modest changes have been made to the reward system but, as noted in Chapter 2, remain hotly debated among management decision-makers. Limited

performance contribution recognition has been introduced over a two-year period, at the time of annual salary reviews. In addition to the across-the-board inflation-linked salary increases, two additional categories have been introduced to determine increase levels – good, and exceptional, contributors.

The scheme is not a formal incentive programme. It is a recognition arrangement, intended to signal acknowledgement of particular contribution levels. It is recognised that the levels involved are not likely to act as a retention device in the case of people leaving for higher material rewards elsewhere. While top management's intention has been to communicate a positive message, there has been some negative reaction. Dissatisfaction has centred on things like who is included and why, and at an individual level, debate on issues such as why only good and not exceptional. Some senior management team members express anxieties about differentiation on the grounds that pay-for-performance may run counter to the overriding principles likely to typify not-for-profit organisations internationally.

Making the global pay bill spend effective

> 'The driving ambition [in BT] is to make every experience simple and complete.'

Commercially-oriented multinationals like **BT** have been applying change principles to reward management as part of aspirations to transform the organisation – in BT's case to become a global ICT company. The driving ambition is to make every experience simple and complete. The organisation is on a journey towards a single pan-BT reward system. The intention is not to increase or decrease reward expenditure but to make what is spent as effective as possible. The reward system is intended to:

❖ be simple and complete, matched to the brand promise

❖ accentuate transparency through standardisation and access to information

❖ create 'maturity' in the employment relationship – a change imperative

❖ provide cost leadership – in internal performance and to the external market (a shift from a traditionally inwardly-focused perspective).

The basis of the reward system is 18 role-based job families. This is accompanied by detailed specification of what and how employees are each expected to perform. Business-to-individual scorecards are aligned with the new accent on transparency – do this and this is what you will receive. Pay positioning within the job-family ranges is a reflection of hierarchical positions, and bonus distributions and benefits are also matched in this way. The system has already been applied to all employee groups outside the UK, including workforces in companies acquired to reinforce the new global ICT corporate profile (in the UK so far only managers and professional-level employees are covered). There is commonality of practice in grading and performance-related reward principles; actual compensation levels are market-matched country by country.

Employee reaction has been positive – a biennial staff attitude survey has produced a positive reaction to how performance affects reward and to perceptions of market match. However, as in HelpAge International, controversy has had to be managed, although BT's management remains resolute on driving change through. There remains a core said to be fundamentally opposed to differentiating between employees on performance grounds – the task is to reduce this to a minimum. And there have been mixed views among managers at the decision to make the reward systems (and the full details of the job-family structure and associated reward packages) accessible to all employees covered by the arrangements via the corporate intranet. However, the corporate view is that to realise a true performance-based approach, complete transparency is necessary 'so people can see how it will affect pay'.

Self-service and standardisation technology

As in the case of BT, performance-aligned reward management is linked with moves to increase standardisation across worldwide operations by **Honeywell**, a diversified technology and manufacturing organisation with 110,000 employees across 90 countries. Its product markets include aerospace products and services, control technologies for buildings, homes and industry, automotive products, and specialty materials.

Honeywell has also embarked on an HR transformation strategy where, according to a European reward strategy architect, 'technology is a key enabler, underpinning generalist business partnering capabilities'. With an emphasis on self-service HR management, major investments have been made in technology and shared services, with the ambition of improving quality while achieving cost reductions. Technology is also helping to 'drive global process and programme standardisation'.

The global performance and development system offers 'comprehensive information, and guidance on performance and development' across the organisation's worldwide operations online. The system is accessed via the Internet or corporate intranet with personal ID and access code. The global performance and development system offers self-service capabilities to both employees and managers.

* Employees are able to update individual performance goals, results and career profile throughout the year.

* They can also use the system to set goals for the year ahead, and receive performance assessment; after discussion, employees submit goals for approval by their line manager.

* The website explains the tasks to be undertaken, coupled with step-by-step instructions, performance planning hints and practical information.

* Links are provided also to additional tools and resources associated with employment and career management, as well as offering links to training.

In addition to enabling interaction between employees and their supervisors on 'goals management' and performance assessment, system functionality triggers a second-level manager review of initial judgements. Managers also have the means to have information transferred automatically to the Honeywell global compensation planning tool, to inform pay decisions:

* Managers are able to view and plan for all components of total compensation.

* The system integrates intelligence such as pay guidelines, spend, internal and market data, as well as individual performance and potential ratings with the planning process, providing modelling and analytical capability.

* Reporting facilities synthesising the outcome of individualised process and rollup information are available using the online system, with output at various organisation, function, management and executive levels.

* The system configuration offers the flexibility to tailor support to country- and/or business-specific requirements.

Bravo and My Total Rewards

A further web-enabled system known as Bravo adds to the performance and compensation planning architecture at Honeywell. Bravo is used to reward and recognise employee contribution over and above an individual's annual goals, with direct links online to a set of five initiatives management are pursuing as part of the overall corporate strategy. Bravo payouts are normalised, taking into account foreign exchange values as well as cost-of-living differentials. For example, paying a $1,000 recognition award to an individual employee in India could be divisive, given total compensation relativities within that employment system.

Currently only available in the United States but planned for extension to cover all operations worldwide, Honeywell has invested in a further online tool that provides a personalised communication to employees on the value of each component of their reward package (direct pay, benefits and other programmes) known as My Total Rewards. A barrier to worldwide application is harmonisation of benefits where multiple systems exist, reflecting local institutional and related norms.

Performance and reward management life online

The approach to technology-enabled reward management in Honeywell is justified as part of a more general trend where individuals are becoming increasingly acclimatised to online activities, for example, Internet banking and other personal financially-related activities. And for a company operating across multiple networks internationally, managerial benefits are significant. For example, a manager may have direct reports in ten different countries – the performance and reward management system supports continuous virtual dialogue without time-

Figure 6 ✦ **Extract from Honeywell's global performance development system web pages**

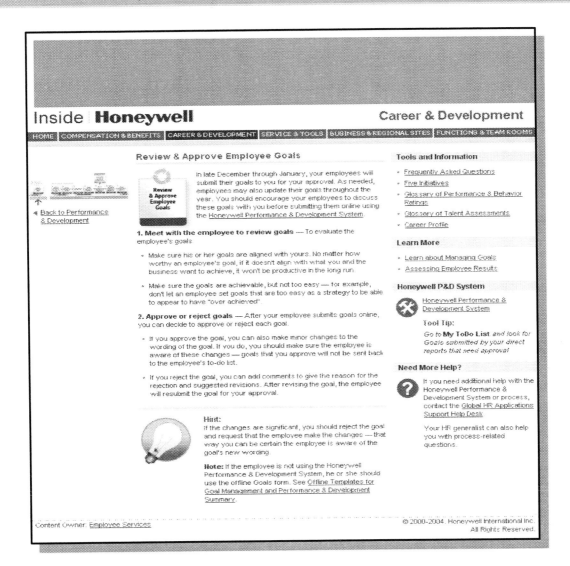

consuming and costly travelling. And Honeywell reports benefits from the vantage point of corporate reward strategy designers seeking to maximise the potential inherent in pay systems, in particular (as referred to in Chapters 1 and 2) to iron out differences in practice worldwide.

> People talk about the 'special character' of the pay arrangements in their part of the world. But we're challenging that. A technology-enabled reward management system needs to limit if not eradicate differences – managerial practice needs to be aligned with the architecture, particularly bearing in mind the scale of corporate investment to develop and implement such a facility.

Rationalisation of reward systems to match global standard practices

Technology is empowering corporate designers of reward systems in their concern to rationalise the range of terms available,

because 'The programme won't accommodate departures from the standards being laid down corporately.'

As an IT business, it comes as no surprise that e-enabled total reward is reported in Hewlett-Packard.

> The way we want to deliver HR ideally is through the web, so that you give the rationale, the philosophy, and the detail of HR programmes to employees through the web. And they can access and work with them directly.

> Our employees get an online total rewards guide. What does 'total rewards' mean in HP? It starts off explaining what it is – here's the total reward framework, made up of the following elements, any one of which the employee can click on to get detailed printouts.

> Likewise, you give managers tools: you do it through the web. So, on ... the performance review process, the salary review process, first of all, you train managers on

that on the web. They go on to the web and go through a training programme. You give them the tools to do the job – on the web. And they interact with their employees – on the web. And then at the end of it they have a face-to-face and ensure that the communication is correct. But so much of it is on the web.

> '...the self-service mindset may take some time to embed in regions...where face-to-face interaction is very important to individuals.'

However, the self-service mindset may take some time to embed in regions (the Latin countries, for example, described earlier) where face-to-face interaction is very important to individuals. It may also be the case that workforces in less technology-focused organisations may take longer to develop an affinity with online management, in spite of the increasing experience of technology-enabled transactions in private life. And there still remains the issue of communicating some difficult messages that employees may need time to get used to. As our Hewlett-Packard interviewee put it:

While changing the methods of delivering performance and reward management, the company has been struggling to change the words. It changed the practice four years ago. But changing the words it's finding difficult.

REWARDING THE TRANSATLANTIC DIMENSION

Blending considerations of international mobility with current performance alignment aspirations, in addition to pursuing managerial strategies for simplifying through standardising reward management principles, a major concern exercising corporate specialists consulted as part of the research for this report falls under the rubric of 'transatlantic comparative tensions'.

Organisations such as Cadbury Schweppes, Lloyds TSB and National Grid Transco, to name but three UK-headquartered multinationals, find creativity is a prerequisite in managing the competing demands of securing and retaining key skills matched to business demands for knowledge mobilisation without undermining overall integrity of the compensation regime. These appear to be issues of substance, not attributable to 'cultural differences':

Once a candidate has made it as far as engaging seriously in negotiating an employment contract to work at senior level, necessitating a transnational relocation, issues such as culture go on the back burner. The focus becomes (for the individual) the package and 'environment' and (for the company) can we match their aspirations?

The opportunities for executives in the US are so much greater than for their UK equivalents. So there are two clubs the American inpatriates expect to belong to. One is the UK; the other is the USA. 'Create a package that

reflects that I'm in 'this' club and in 'this' club too, and prove it to the world.'

And it is not just 'deal-breaking' economic factors that some US candidates bring to contract negotiations that are problematic: for example, individuals who hold multi-million-dollar restricted stock holdings. Individual aspirations surface like being given a job title that, as one corporate HR professional we interviewed explained, if accepted, 'would have ripples across the organisation', in terms of perceived status inconsistencies. There are 'hygiene factors' based on extracting key talent from a US employment market setting: tax, shares, medical. Assumptions among some candidates surrounding fringe benefits, such as covering the cost of children's education, family medical insurance coverage, etc are also considered primarily a US 'inpatriate' issue.

RECOMMENDATIONS FOR ACTION

We rounded off Chapter 2 by looking at corporate objectives and the implications for international reward management design. To complete Chapter 3, we compare these principles against reported practice in managing employee reward and recognition internationally.

Objective 1: securing skill sets to perform across diverse settings

Pragmatism in the pursuit of this strategic goal appears to be in evidence, whether related to assigning individuals across international borders or in the detailed application of reward policies across multi-local settings.

❖ Citigroup's principle of treating people fairly, offering a rich experience – but not a financial killing – to the internationally mobile is one way of summarising the position.

❖ Another is Unilever's emphasis on integrating reward management with the identification of high-performers and high potential, where standards for determining pay levels are set corporately, but line managers are expected to be fully accountable for their detailed application locally, conditions permitting.

Local managements are expected to own and manage the budgetary consequences and to be held accountable – up the line, not to HR specialists – for their actions in this regard.

So we see that there is a common thread in efforts to transform not the corporate reward management architecture but the *leadership* applied to facilitate its application. Balancing cost–performance factors pragmatically, large commercial multinationals appear willing to set extrinsic rewards at competitive levels to attract and retain employees who demonstrate sustained high performance combined with potential for further development. Financial constraints (and trustee-principals' expectations regarding employee motivators) limiting the tangible elements of the effort–reward bargain raise challenges that bring to light qualitatively different leadership demands in not-for-profit enterprises operating across settings equally in competition for skills and knowledge of the highest calibre.

> **Action**: Specify and build corporate ownership for corporately aligned reward management standards, supporting 'accountable' leadership development to deliver consistent outcomes while respecting alternative routes to their achievement.

Objective 2: facilitating mobility of people and knowledge whose success is tied in with contribution to corporate performance

At the level of principle, concern continues to be expressed when corporate HR specialists are asked to compare the costs of mobilising executives and families internationally, estimated to cost *two to three times more than it would cost to employ a local*. Judgements are more sanguine, however, when reflecting on detailed practice, including (a) increased variability along the dimension of mobility, and (b) determination not to 'subsidise' expatriation that cannot be accounted for in terms of strict commercial benefits.

> '...migration from simple packages of base, plus benefits, plus expatriate package to terms comprising base, plus benefits, plus incentives appears to have relieved the pressures some organisations were describing even as recently as five years ago.'

The perceived general migration from simple packages of base, plus benefits, plus expatriate package to terms comprising base, plus benefits, plus incentives appears to have relieved the pressures some organisations were describing even as recently as five years ago. Incentive-based payments may be afforded in common across organisational networks, whether the employees are contracted for on expatriate or local/national terms – they are just tax-equalised in the former case. Computation of terms for mobilising individuals may be described in fixed sums (a figure of some £200,000 was used as an illustration of the average executive long-term mobility on-cost) in place of the traditional multiple of salary, with incentives acting to provide a dampening effect.

Possibly storing up greater medium-term risk of employee disengagement are situations in which organisations have embarked on a corporate transition, stripping back value distribution among the global workforce to satisfy short-term corporate governance demands as the organisation's competitive ethos has altered radically, but where, for the present, the words do not match the actions.

> **Action**: Approach the detailed application of international assignment terms from a 'fact base' that matches investment costs with clearly specified accountability-for-performance outcomes, communicating the implications transparently.

Objective 3: establishing and sustaining comparability in multinational reward management practice, using common principles while allowing for context-based interpretation of the detail

Organisations such as BT have made significant investments in setting a common framework to underpin the 'more mature' performance–reward relationship aspired to managerially between the organisation and workforce around the world. Essentially, this may give substance to notions of global reward strategy implied by practitioner survey data. Then, as witnessed in organisations such as Cadbury Schweppes, pay is fairly aggressively and closely aligned with sustained high performance, but tied in as closely as possible to local market rates.

As we have seen throughout this report, reward management complexities are amplified when operating across international networks. Judgements are necessary to distinguish between what some respondents have termed 'genuine internationalists' and people working for international companies in a local environment. Common frameworks such as the BT job families architecture facilitate comparability (although line managers may need educating as to the benefits of transparency in some cases) while specifying quantum levels against local benchmarks. As in the Honeywell example, where a $1,000 Bravo award in India could distort local comparisons, care is necessary when cascading corporate schemes that reflect marked difference in market practice. However, there are situations where the local benchmark itself is distorted by 'a lot of quasi-expatriate packages' that inflate the rates paid locally by multinationals (eg circumstances known to the author in Singapore). Comparability in terms of principles of equity and universal treatment across the workforce may give rise to debate when experimenting with reward management innovations, involving differentiation among individuals, as indicated in the HelpAge International case. And although efforts to align corporate and reward management strategies are increasingly in evidence, as with the Unilever Level 1 population, institutional contingent factors may continue to limit final convergence.

> **Action**: constitute an architecture for international reward management that supports the accountability and performance standards set corporately, enabling local 'self-service' access that fosters understanding and flexibility of application.

Objective 4: maintaining reward levels and practices regarded as reasonable on both sides of the effort–reward nexus

The transregional review opened up a vista of the ways organisational aspiration and practice may again be judged directionally, not finally, convergent due to a complex array of cultural and institutional phenomena. On the other hand, though, multinational managements appear to be increasingly adept at managing people and reward factors, albeit with more experimentation than determinism, provided the actors are open to living with complexity and hybrid management practices. On reasonableness, as one respondent said:

> I'd like to say that the managers in the business, and hopefully everybody in the organisation, cares about other people. Treats them with dignity, with respect. Goes out of their way to take account of problems that individuals may face either in their personal life or their business life. And responds to that in a civilised and compassionate way.

The observed use of technology – at one level offering self-service transparency to employees and efficient service support facilities to managers, at another level acting as the motor powering simplification and standardising initiatives driven from the corporate centre – remains charged with interesting potential, the results of which remain to be seen in the years to come.

> **Action**: create the conditions for continuous dialogue between all members of the multinational, to identify ways in which aspirations and priorities around the effort–reward nexus are balanced so that all stakeholders feel treated respectfully, while committing to realistic deliverables.

THE FUTURE OF INTERNATIONAL REWARD AND RECOGNITION

4

❖ **Managerial choices and reward management consequences.**

❖ **Agency, transaction costs, resource-based and institutional factors.**

❖ **Managerial processes and style.**

❖ **The transnational issue of deferred reward.**

❖ **Skills at the multinational core and periphery.**

To conclude, we speculate on possible future developments in international reward and recognition strategy, assuming the continuation of currently emerging trends.

Carefully defined reward management design and its application across multinational operations has an important ongoing role as a pillar of the employment relationship:

❖ communicating corporate intentions to *discourage* performance perceived as contributing negatively to the governing purpose of the enterprise

❖ sharing successes achieved in networking knowledge profitably.

In the *CIPD Guide to International Management Development* (Harris and Dickmann, 2005), a companion to this volume, attention is drawn to the need for 'balanced dialogue' between managers and the high-performing people they wish to engage in international operations, substituting for a unitary organisational perspective. This imperative for 'balance' and 'dialogue' between the parties is writ large in the interrelational bargaining around the effort–reward nexus.

A BALANCED DIALOGUE IN INTERNATIONAL REWARD AND RECOGNITION SYSTEMS

Viewing HR management strategy in systems terms, people management represents a set of connected things (or parts) making up a complex whole – aspects that together form a network or mechanism, for example, operated to achieve specific purposeful objectives.

Research evidence gathered to inform this report has been used to make a case for international reward and recognition policy-makers to weigh corporate considerations for strategy design and implementation alongside diverse human capital perspectives. Assuming scope for dialogue guided by such factors, and looking ahead, continuities as well as novel features may arise calling for the attention of policy-makers and researchers alike.

It has been argued that multinational organisation managements are placing an overriding emphasis on generating and mobilising knowledge with a view to more integrated organisational development internationally. Integration is prized as offering improved potential to grow international operations. This may be to increase corporate profits for distribution to financial investors in commercial firms, or in cost-effective application of scarce resources in not-for-profit enterprises. Such a governing objective implies an imperative shared across all multinational organisations to secure skills cost-effectively, redirecting attention to managerial initiatives at the effort–reward nexus.

Ongoing attention among those concerned with directing international reward management, as an integrated feature of multinational HR management systems, is therefore likely to be directed to balancing two considerations involving skills and costs.

This core aim must be examined to help in deciding how, if accepted as a universal goal, it can be associated with choices about the role that the management of rewards can play as part of future multinational organisation strategy and practice.

STRATEGIC GOALS: MANAGERIAL CHOICE CONSIDERATIONS

At one level, the focus is the basic task of securing, keeping, developing, and motivating individuals and groups of individuals under an employment relationship. However, as Hendry (2003) argues, a more strategic interpretation adds an important caveat. The managerial rationale for getting, keeping, developing, and motivating employees is assumed as carrying with it the implication that management wishes to exercise control over the skills so engaged (that is, to deploy people to work purposefully on managerially defined tasks) in different ways and to different degrees.

> '...[it] is assumed...that management wishes to exercise control over the skills so engaged (that is, to deploy people to work purposefully on managerially defined tasks) in different ways and to different degrees.'

❖ In the case of skills that are perceived as less central to achievement of the organisation's purpose, traditional economic theory (prices and markets) may inform managerial action.

❖ External market forces – in terms of supply of and demand for labour – may be used to drive down the cost of employing people to serve the organisation's needs. There are indications that this approach is being pursued by multinationals corporately through offshoring and related initiatives, as a strategy for managing skills perceived as non-core.

❖ However, there may be significant modifiers due to the need to apply the strategy in different locations and organisational settings across national borders.

Strategies, business systems and talent deal-making

Evidence presented in this report implies an expectation that ongoing attention will be needed in order to manage interaction between the specificities of corporate strategy and business system characteristics. 'Regime shopping' (Traxler and Woitech, 2000) becomes more complicated in an environment where norms and values endorsed by elites in certain 'varieties' of capitalism (Whitley, 2000) are not completely in sync with those of the multinational.

In contrast, the approach management adopts to controlling the skills felt to be central to the achievement of corporate purpose may involve the political choice to limit the effect of external economic market forces. While general deregulation of historically 'inflexible' labour markets appears set to continue, as witnessed in the European data contrasting countries such as Germany and Spain, the pace will tend to vary: final convergence may remain elusive in some employment systems. And the same considerations may continue to apply at the micro level, when transatlantic senior executive 'deals' are negotiated, with consequences for longer-term human capital perceptions of comparability criteria.

Agency, transaction costs, resource-based and institutional factors

Managerial choices in favour of attempted control of the HR management system may be perceived as being informed by the resource-based approach to competitive strategy, where attempts are made to combine human capital resource and organisational systems into strategic bundles that enable the organisation to prosper in market-influenced competition for scarce resources. Institutionalised experience of reciprocity in networked exchanges may reinforce a sense that performance potential will be realised on either side of the effort–reward nexus in the medium term.

However, given corporate governance preoccupations, the perceived shortening of product and service relationship lifecycles, and the costs of the employment relationship all of which take time to bear fruit, it is possible that agency and transaction costs thinking will continue. Contingent reward management practices may be followed as consistently as transnational business systems considerations will allow. The political choice to try to insulate the firm from external economic market forces by creating internal markets, where seniority is the contingency, is rejected – likewise, simple acquiescence in the view that market forces constitute a 'black box'. The role of management is to proactively organise the many micro-level economic transactions between each employee and the organisation's demand for his or her skills to minimise the cost involved. An appropriate bundle of incentives and accounting mechanisms will be required to ensure that agents remain focused on organisational rather than personal or wider social concerns.

An emphasis on management process and style

Neither ideology carries easier managerial practice implications. And the emphasis on leadership surfacing in North American employment system commentary may be a response to this. Attempting to shift the risks associated with paying premiums to retain skilled resources that form part of a complex network of organisational expertise, through contingent pay systems, requires considerable managerial effort. Managing engagement implies at a minimum matching actions with words.

> 'Retaining the governing emphasis on cost-effectiveness in skills acquisition, adoption of resource-based and institutionally grounded reward management requires skilful management...'

'Patient capital' governance may be passé (Thompson, 2003), as stock market regulation (and its influence on thinking in other sectors) spreads its influence yet further across transnational business systems. Retaining the governing emphasis on cost-effectiveness in skills acquisition, adoption of resource-based and institutionally grounded reward management requires skilful management in order to persuade the employees that their long-term interests are bound up with those of corporate management.

Extending equity-based and other forms of financial reward widely across multinational networks (navigating transnational accounting and taxation regimes) to encourage a workforce orientation to defer gratification in return for a promise of enhanced longer-term economic benefits may represent a tangible example for those willing to innovate.

In addition to providing immediate material benefits to individual 'core' employees, the organisation may also offer development and promotion opportunities that formally signal recognition of organisation members' behavioural contribution – as well as the outcomes of performance – to the corporately designated purpose worldwide.

The transnational problem of deferred reward

Something that has current and ongoing implications for the effort–reward nexus is the question of the more traditional deferred compensation promise (a defined-benefit retirement pension). The gradual erosion of this element of the extrinsic reward package, influencing perceptions well beyond the extent of those enjoying the benefit, has both supporters and detractors:

- ❖ Employees who value portability of accrued economic benefits from employment – with the intention of a multiple-employer career – may be easily persuaded of the merits of change.

- ❖ Those anticipating less elasticity in career locations may need educating in the benefits of performance-related deferred gratification – combining a portfolio of defined-contribution pension credits with equity-based upside and downside.

In particular, individuals in socially-oriented employment systems geared to family income protection, and those still migrating from an era where economic undertakings by 'the authorities' were deemed suspect, may require more sensitive handling by multinational managements.

Rewarding core and peripheral skill sets

Multinational managements are likely to continue to face tensions in the quest to control skill types – defined on a scale between core and peripheral, depending on how central they are perceived to be to management's goals – and controlling the costs of securing these applied skills to a greater or lesser extent within the organisation or through the external economic market. Even where an agency–transaction-cost-informed strategy prevails, managerial reliance on specific reward approaches reflecting detailed decision-making – in dynamic interaction with employees and external factors – may become embedded over time.

Tradition or custom may result in such practice bundles prevailing until a performance gap opens up (most likely due to an external shock, such as additional shareholder pressure to enhance returns and competitive pressures to satisfy consumer demands) which forces a reappraisal of the specific reward strategy choices. Managerial agency becomes a response to the risk of organisational failure.

SUMMARY AND IMPLICATIONS FOR FUTURE PRACTICE   **5**

To conclude with a summary of discernible trends in international reward and recognition, the evidence reviewed for this report suggests the need for:

❖ continuing managerial resolve to tackle underperformance which past practice may have ignored or overlooked. Because it can now no longer be accounted for, future initiatives are likely to test managerial skill and resolve

❖ ongoing attention to realise the potential for standardisation in pay systems and relate to other reward elements where opportunities arise.

❖ further investment in self-service IT-enabled reward management systems architecture

❖ ongoing enhanced managerial communications around transitioning effort–reward bargaining, and improved managerial education to facilitate this

❖ ongoing pragmatism around expatriate reward management, along a dimension registering multiple categories of performance-mediated international mobility

❖ increased reliance on 'insider' talent, while wrestling with comparability issues

❖ detecting opportunities and threats around notions of deferred compensation

❖ a 'reality check' comparing directional and final practice convergence.

APPENDIX: RESEARCH METHODOLOGY

SOURCES OF IDEAS AND ISSUES FOR INVESTIGATION

The project began with the opportunity to solicit ideas and priorities for research in dialogue with a cross-section of HR professionals who attended a joint networking meeting of the CIPD International and Reward Forums in autumn 2004. This was helpful in giving us a good idea of the current hot topics specialists were facing in their day-to-day work that were associated with the design and management of reward in a transnational environment. Preliminary results were tested at the 22nd European Association for Personnel Management conference held in Dublin in May 2005, and at a CIPD research symposium in July 2005. Consolidated findings were cascaded, with some case study presentations, at a joint International and Reward Forums meeting in December 2005.

A range of literature was reviewed during the winter of 2004 and spring 2005 in order to find out about the debates taking place among the international academic community (writing in English). Hypotheses from the theoretical literature were examined, alongside commentary reporting on the issues empirical researchers said they had uncovered during (mainly) the previous five to six years. The report builds on a previous CIPD publication. Accordingly, the framework and research design builds on the conceptual and empirical foundations laid in the first edition (Perkins and Hendry, 1999a).

DATA COLLECTION

Having decided that a range of 'what?', 'how?', and 'why?' questions required exploration, a mixed-methods approach to data collection was adopted. Interest in trends on what was being done and opinion on how this was influenced and managed suggested that a survey to capture a quantitative data set would be appropriate. To complement this, particularly where it was possible to revisit organisations (or key informants who had shifted organisation) included in the research for the first edition, we conducted a series of conversational interviews with senior HR professionals, as a basis to assemble case-study-style material probing the reasoning behind international reward design and administration. This also enabled more in-depth consideration of corporate strategy developments and perceived influences in the global financial and operating environment likely to impact on future-facing reward strategy developments. The survey was administered during the spring of 2005; interviews were organised and conducted during spring and summer 2005.

> The survey was administered during the spring of 2005; interviews were organised and conducted during spring and summer 2005.'

Population sampling and the online survey

In order to secure a group of respondents willing to complete a survey instrument, it was agreed with the CIPD that an invitation would be circulated among registered members of the International and Reward Forums whose email addresses were held in a CIPD database used for regular communication of forums events and related activity. Once the questionnaire had been designed and pilot tested, a circular email was distributed on two occasions during the spring of 2005 (an initial invitation to participate and a follow-up reminder). Overall, a period of some eight weeks was allocated for those contacted to respond. Although not a random sample, this 'purposive sampling' approach (Black, 1999) had the potential to capture views across a range of practitioners in organisations across the for-profit and not-for-profit sectors, with multinational operations and/or outlook.

Respondents were invited to register and complete the survey online via webpages hosted by an international management consultancy, ORC Worldwide, who invested resources in the web design and technical management of the survey process. One hundred people registered for the survey, and 63 completed responses were eventually received. Although the sample did not reflect random characteristics and the size of the survey dataset was not large enough to make broad statistical generalisations, an interesting and varied set of results emerged offering a basis for reflection on possible trends.

Maylor and Blackmon (2005) note the increasing popularity of 'web surveys'. In accordance with standard practice, potential respondents were directed to a web address where they could link to the survey registration document. Full details of how to register, how to access and respond to the questionnaire, and how to contact members of the research team if necessary to clarify details, were displayed on a webpage (accessed from http://dynasurv.orcww.com/CIPD2005/login.asp). If respondents preferred to complete a paper copy of the questionnaire, they were invited to email the survey manager at ORC Worldwide, supplying name and address, and this was sent to them as an email attachment. Only two respondents requested paper questionnaires, which were supplied.

A tailored survey document was constructed through which registered respondents could complete a computer-assisted set of questions. The survey document was divided up into a series of web pages on which a range of questions were listed. A pilot survey was conducted with respondents in the CIPD and ORC Worldwide, and alterations made to the layout and wording of the survey instrument. Once a respondent had entered data and that page of responses had been 'submitted' by hitting the correct on-screen button, it was saved. The entered data would be available for the respondent to pick up from the page he or she had stopped at when resuming data entry at a later convenient time.

Benefits to respondents were the flexibility with which they could record their input. It was not necessary to complete the survey in a single sitting. Busy people in an office environment may find it challenging to devote 30 minutes to completing a single task, given competing demands on their attention. And it was acknowledged during pilot testing that time for careful reflection was needed on a number of the survey fields, because they asked for opinions on strategic matters. It was therefore important to make the process of completing the questionnaire as user-friendly as possible to encourage respondents to follow the process to complete submission of their data input.

'...the advantage of online data collection instruments is that there is no need to re-enter data, as is necessary when paper questionnaires are used and coded data is then transferred to a computer...'

For survey researchers, the advantage of online data collection instruments is that there is no need to re-enter data, as is necessary when paper questionnaires are used and coded data is then transferred to a computer for analysis. This makes a considerable saving in data-input resources and the risk of data-processing errors – quality control is via the survey design and the

action of respondents. The possible disadvantage of web surveys, using generalised proprietary software, where control may be sacrificed over who answers and how many times they answer (Maylor and Blackmon, 2005), was overcome by a tailored design and by restricting access only to pre-registered respondents who received a password to gain access to their 'personal' online questionnaire. A specialist survey manager at ORC Worldwide with long-standing expertise in both paper-based and web surveys oversaw the entire design, registration and quality control process.

The survey instrument

In addition to personal and corporate demographic and other factual information, the survey was designed across three measurement factors, each exploring a variety of sub-themes, informed by reviewing the literature on aspects of strategic international HR management and associated reward systems. In summary, factors that impact on international reward and recognition design and implementation were explored, complemented by questions regarding local national and internationally mobile employee performance management and reward. A particular influence on the direction and structuring of questioning was a paper in the *International Journal of Human Resource Management* by Bloom, Milkovich and Mitra (2003). Likert-style (1–5) scales were applied to gauge opinions on a range of issues.

An overview of the thematic coverage of the survey is summarised below.

Corporate governing aim(s)

Respondents were asked for their perceptions of the primary and secondary aims of their organisations, with a variety of choices to select from that covered issues associated with shareholder wealth creation, reputation with customers, employment provision, competitiveness in the sector, and corporate citizenship. Respondents could declare item(s) not applicable to their organisation, as necessary. Interestingly, a majority of respondents seemed to feel the need to respond to each of the items listed, ranking them as either primary or secondary (somewhat illogically, given there are only two possible choices to be first or second), with the balance nominally inapplicable.

Overall reward strategy

Respondents were invited to indicate their level of agreement with a series of statements designed to build understanding of the degree to which organisations seek to align people management, and the reward aspects, directly with corporate business strategy. Respondents were also asked for their view on the proposition that the desired aim was to tailor people management to the circumstances in which the organisation operates in its various country subsidiary operations. As a third strand, respondents were asked whether or not their organisation rejected either a wholly corporate or a wholly local approach to managing the reward system, instead perceiving a dynamic framework that reflects experiential learning from operating across a variety of territories of which the corporate headquarters is only one part, and each location is regarded as part of a networked transnational entity.

Developing these themes in a slightly different but complementary direction, respondents were asked for their views on the adoption of common reward system practices, based on 'home-grown' principles, or where the variation across spheres of international operation was accepted, to account for the differences that impact on the employment relationship multinationals enjoy in different countries. As a 'third way', respondents were asked for their views on whether blanket approaches to reward management were regarded as not feasible, given the dynamic pace of development impacting on the organisation, the country of operation, and the global context in which multinational enterprises may learn from operational experience. So, was it the case in their perception that reward strategies continuously evolve?

Respondents were requested to indicate the degree to which they adopt a reactive approach to local regulation and practices, irrespective of whether or not this has adverse consequences for aspirations to align corporate strategy and reward management. Alternatively, respondents could indicate a tendency to explore ways to avoid pressures for locally driven conformity where this is perceived to inhibit the flexibility to achieve alignment. As a further alternative, respondents were asked to comment on whether or not their organisation preferred to match reward system management practice to a range of contexts in which it has to be applied (where corporate headquarters ranks alongside the collection of transnational operations) as a means to achieve corporate strategy. Finally, respondents were invited to indicate whether their organisation would seriously consider the merits of employing people directly in countries (or withdrawing operations or 'bussing in' cross-border workers) where they felt the local context left the organisation feeling unable to manage rewards in accordance with corporate strategy.

International reward strategy and practice

Respondents were presented with a series of factors and institutional actors that might be perceived as influences on reward strategy and the management of pay progression. They were asked to rank the degree of influence on a five-point scale, from 'no influence' to 'influencing strategy to a very great extent'. Respondents were asked to indicate whether or not they gathered intelligence on managerial and workforce views on the reward system across the organisation. They were asked for their views on the degree to which the organisation linked rewards to performance appraisal – in philosophy, in performance, or in perception ('always', 'sometimes', 'never'). Finally, a series of questions were posed with possible answers regarding current issues associated with rewarding individuals required to be internationally mobile.

A series of descriptive statistics were generated with SPSS statistical software, using summary displays (graphs and tables) to indicate general patterns and trends discernible in the data set, and informing the empirical analysis reported in this research publication. Information on respondents and their organisations is summarised below.

THE SURVEY SAMPLE – SUMMARY DEMOGRAPHIC RESULTS

Respondent characteristics

Respondents were fairly evenly divided between males (49.2%) and females (50.8%). They were well qualified academically and professionally. Almost half (47.6%) had a postgraduate qualification – in the case of almost a quarter (22.2%), a professional qualification was their highest qualification. The most frequently occurring age band was 30–39 (38.1% of respondents), with those in the 40–49 and 50–59 age-bands almost evenly divided at 23.0% and 27.0% respectively. Two-thirds of the sample said they had British citizenship; the remainder were divided between various mainland European countries, Australia, South Africa and North America. Almost all respondents (93.7%) were work-based in European countries. A little under half of all respondents (46%) had worked in two or more countries over the course of their career to date. And just over half (51.8%) declared themselves competent in at least one language in addition to their native tongue – a quarter (25.4%) said two or more languages.

> Most respondents were HR functional specialists...employed by their current organisation for 7½ years on average...evenly based across the [manufacturing and service sectors although]...the for-profit sector dominated...'

Most respondents were HR functional specialists (92.5%), 35% of whom had a corporate policy role, and over 40% were in divisional roles, either as specialists (25.4%) or HR generalists (17.5%). Only just over 3% had country specialist/management roles (19% described themselves as 'function heads', one as a managing director and one as a consultant – most could probably be counted under a 'corporate policy-maker' label). Respondents had been employed by their current organisation for 7½ years on average (4 years median). Respondents were evenly based across the range of sectors (including government and voluntary sector): manufacturing and services. The for-profit sector dominated, however, with 86% of respondents.

Organisational characteristics

Respondents' organisations tended to be large: 54% employed more than 10,000 people corporately (27% 1,000–10,000). However, 10% employed up to 999 people. Corporate headquarters were located predominantly either in Europe (65.1%) or North America (28.6%), with 3.2% Japanese-parented firms (1.6% in each case for the Middle East and Central or South America). Organisation structure declared by respondents was divided 33.3% in each case between global lines of business and a series of geographically dispersed divisions. And 17.5% of respondents described their enterprises as organised along traditional functional lines, the remaining 15.9% indicating some form of matrix operation combining functional and geographical areas. Although just under 20% of respondents said their firms had operated internationally for fewer than 10 years, a majority were well-established multinationals: 18.6% for 10–19 years; 27.1% for 20– 49 years; and 30.5% for 50 years or more (5.1% said their organisations did not operate across national borders). On average, including the country of origin, respondents said their organisations had offices or plants in nearly 44 countries (21.5 median).

Organisational case interviews

A sample of senior HR executives was interviewed since 'interviews are suggested to be the best way to gain insights into the culture, organization, and activity of executives' (Unseem, 1995, cited in Guest and King, 2004; p409). The qualitative sample was similarly purposive, replicating, where possible, the case study organisations investigated in 1999. Some cluster sampling was undertaken so that not-for-profit, banking and financial services, energy, fast-moving manufactured consumer goods, hi-tech, publishing, retailing, and telecommunications sectors were all included. Additionally, senior-level individuals in international management consultancies were interviewed so that we could learn about the contemporary issues clients were bringing to them. Interviews were conducted with respondents in the following 16 organisations: BG Holdings, Boots, Cable and Wireless, Cadbury Schweppes, Citigroup, Hay Group, HelpAge International, Hewlett-Packard, Honeywell, Lloyds TSB, Mercer HR Consulting, NationalGrid, Prudential, Reed Elsevier, Shell, Watson Wyatt.

Interview guide themes

Themes were derived from reviewing the literature on aspects of strategic international HR management and associated reward systems, as well as initial findings from the survey.

Respondents were asked to describe the distinctive features of the way their enterprise is organised, in particular how 'global' the substance and process of organisation seems to be. They were questioned on the issue of changes in governance and organisation over the preceding five years, and the underlying influences. Implications for employee reward were discussed.

On reward management in general, interviewees were asked to articulate the philosophy that underpins employee reward management in their enterprise, and to comment on whether or not they had come across evidence that this philosophy had changed in the past five years. Views on possible influences on changing reward strategy and practice were probed for. Issues were probed regarding the consistency of application of reward

principles across all units of the organisation, all countries in which it operates, and to all levels and categories of employees.

A view was solicited as to how satisfied corporate management, on the one hand, and divisional/country managers, on the other, were judged to be with the way the employee reward system was currently structured and administered.

> 'Respondents were asked to comment on the issue of reward and recognition systems reflecting a so-called "global corporate mindset".'

Details of the elements of employee reward internationally were discussed with interviewees, and then perceptions were drawn out of the main problems currently faced in managing employee performance, reward and recognition internationally. Respondents were asked to comment on the issue of reward and recognition systems reflecting a so-called 'global corporate mindset'.

Finally, respondents were invited to discuss current issues surrounding the reward management considerations associated with business needs to mobilise talented people across international borders.

Qualitative data recording and analysis

All interviews were recorded and transcribed (with copies sent to respondents to confirm they were happy with the contents representing their views). The qualitative data set was coded using themes identified in the literature review, combined with emergent themes from the survey and based on a careful reading and re-reading of the interview transcripts. Sensitising concepts such as 'accountability', 'standardisation', 'practice transferability', and 'centralisation' surfaced as significant. Additionally, a data reduction and interpretation approach based on reported 'issues and processes' was followed (Quinn Patton, 2002). Interviewees' comments on what were perceived as important policy challenges and processes for enacting changes to HR management and reward strategy were compared with one another. Change in practice was a repeated theme throughout the interviews, irrespective of business sector, as were pressures associated with corporate governance developments on the one hand, and, on the other, transnational employment market pressures for recruiting, retaining and encouraging high performance among talented people.

REFERENCES

ANAKWE, U. P. (2002)

'Human resource management practices in Nigeria: challenges and insights'. *International Journal of Human Resource Management*, Vol 13, No 7, November; pp1042–59.

ASHBY, T. (2006)

'Nigerian militants threaten new oil attacks'. *Reuters*. 18 January. http://www.theepochtimes.com/news/6-1-18/37088.html [Acccessed 29 January 2006].

BARNEY, J., WRIGHT, M. and KETCHEN, D. J. (2001)

'The resource-based view of the firm: ten years after 1991'. *Journal of Management*, No 27; pp625–41.

BLACK, T. R. (1999)

Doing Quantitative Research in the Social Sciences: An integrated approach to research design, measurement and statistics. London: Sage.

BLOOM, M., MILKOVICH, G. T. and MITRA, A. (2003)

'International compensation: learning from how managers respond to variation in local host contexts'. *International Journal of Human Resource Management*, Vol 14, No 8, pp1350–67.

BRADLEY, P., HENDRY, C. and PERKINS, S. J. (1999)

'Global or multi-local? The significance of international values in reward strategy', in: BREWSTER, C. and HARRIS, H. (eds) *International HRM: Contemporary issues in Europe*. London: Routledge; pp120–42.

BRISCOE, D. R. and SCHULER, R. S. (2004)

International Human Resource Management: Policy and practice for the global enterprise. 2nd ed. London: Routledge.

BROWN, D. (2001)

Reward Strategies: From intent to impact. London: Chartered Institute of Personnel and Development.

BUDHWAR, P. S. and BOYNE, G. (2004)

'Human resource management in the Indian public and private sectors: an empirical comparison'. *International Journal of Human Resource Management*, Vol 15, No 2, March; pp346–70.

BUDHWAR, P. S. and KHATRI, N. (2001)

'HRM in context: applicability of HRM models in India'. *International Journal of Cross-Cultural Management*, Vol 1, No 3; pp333–56.

DOWLING, P. J., WELCH, D. E. and SCHULER, R. S. (1999)

International Human Resource Management: Managing people in a multinational context. 3rd ed. Cincinnati, OH: South Western College Publishing.

DOWLING, P. J. and WELCH, D. E. (2004)

International Human Resource Management: Managing people in a multinational context. 4th ed. London: Thomson.

ECONOMIST [ONLINE] (2004)

'A lift from India: how offshoring gives British companies an advantage over the competition'. 4 March. Available at: http://economist.com/displaystory.cfm?story_id=E1_NQRNNPT [Accessed 18 January 2006].

EDWARDS, T., ALMOND, P. and CLARK, I. (2005)

'Reverse diffusion in US multinationals: barriers from the American business system'. *Journal of Management Studies*, Vol 42, No 6, September; pp1261–86.

ELVIRA, M. M. and DAVILA, A. (2005A)

'Introducing the Special research issue on human resource management in Latin America'. *International Journal of Human Resource Management*, Vol 16, No 12, December; pp2164–72.

ELVIRA, M. M. and DAVILA, A. (2005B)

'Emergent directions for human resource management research in Latin America'. *International Journal of Human Resource Management*, Vol 16, No 12, December; pp2265–82.

FARASHAHI, M., HAFSI, T. and MOLZ, R. (2005)

'Institutionalized norms of conducting research and social realities: a research synthesis of empirical works from 1983 to 2002'. *International Journal of Management Reviews*, Vol 7, No 1, March; pp1–24.

FEDERATION OF EUROPEAN EMPLOYERS (2005)

Pay in Europe 2005. London: Federation of European Employers.

GHOSHAL, S. and BARTLETT, C. A. (1998)

Managing Across Borders: The transnational solution. 2nd ed. London: Random House.

GOODHERHAM, P. N. and NORDHAUG, O. (2003)

International Management: Cross-boundary challenges. Oxford: Blackwell.

GOURLAY, S. (2006)

'Knowledge management and international human resources management', in: EDWARDS, T. and REES, C. (eds) *International Human Resource Management: Globalization, national systems and multinational companies*. Harlow: Financial Times/Prentice Hall; pp151–71.

GUEST, D. E. and KING, Z. (2004)

'Power, innovation and problem-solving: the personnel managers' three steps to heaven?'. *Journal of Management Studies*, Vol 41, No 3, May; pp 401–23.

HALL, P. A. and SOSKICE, D. (2001)

Varieties of Capitalism: The Institutional Foundations of Comparative Advantage. Oxford: Oxford University Press.

HARRIS, H. and DICKMANN, M. (2005)

CIPD Guide: International Management Development. London: Chartered Institute of Personnel and Development.

HENDRY, C. (2003)

'Applying employment systems theory to the analysis of national models of HRM'. *International Journal of Human Resource Management*, Vol 4, No 8, December; pp1430–42.

HOFSTEDE, G. (2003)

Culture's Consequence: Comparing values, behaviours, institutions and organizations across nations. 2nd ed. London: Sage.

HONG CHUNG, L., GIBBONS, P. T. and SCHOCH, H. P. (2006)

'The management of information and managers in subsidiaries of multinational corporations'. *British Journal of Management*, Vol 17, No 2, pp153–65.

JENSEN, M. C. and MECKLING, W. H. (1976)

'Theory of the firm: managerial behavior, agency costs, and ownership structure'. *Journal of Financial Economics*, Vol 3, No 4; pp305–60. Online version also available at http:// ssrn.com/abstract=94043 [Accessed 14 June 2006].

KAMOCHE, K. (2002)

'Introduction: human resource management in Africa'. *International Journal of Human Resource Management*, Vol 13, No 7, November; pp993–7.

KAYE, L. (1999)

'Strategic human resources management in Australia: the human cost'. *International Journal of Manpower*, Vol 20, No 8, December; pp577–87.

KESSLER, I. (2001)

'Reward system choices', in: STOREY, J. *Human Resource Management: A critical text*. 2nd ed. London: Thomson Learning; pp206–31.

KESSLER, I. (2005)

'Remuneration systems', in: BACH. S. (ed.) *Managing Human Resources: Personnel management in transition*. Oxford: Blackwell; pp 317–45.

MAMMAN, A. and REES, C. J. (2005)

'Australian managerial attitudes towards employee relations: a comparison with the British National Survey'. *Asia Pacific Journal of Human Resources*, Vol 43, No 3; pp381–403.

MAYLOR, H. and BLACKMON, K. (2005)

Researching Business and Management. Basingstoke: Palgrave Macmillan.

MERCER HUMAN RESOURCE CONSULTING (2005)

Expatriate and Third-Country Nationals Benefits Survey. Geneva: Mercer Human Resource Consulting.

MICHAELS, E., HANDFIELD-JONES, H. and AXELROD, B. (2001)

The War for Talent. Boston, MA: Harvard Business School Press.

MILKOVICH, G. T. and NEWMAN, J. M. (1989)

Compensation. 2nd ed. Plano, TX: Business Publications.

MORGAN, G. (2001)

'The multinational firm: organizing across institutional and national divides', in: MORGAN, G., KRISTENSEN, P. H. and WHITLEY, R. (eds) *The Multinational Firm: Organizing across institutional and national divides*. Oxford: Oxford University Press; pp1–24.

NORTH, D. C. (1990)

Institutions, Institutional Change, and Economic Performance. Cambridge: Cambridge University Press.

OXFORD ENGLISH DICTIONARY (LATEST EDITION)

Oxford: Oxford University Press.

PEOPLE MANAGEMENT (2004)

'Shell chairman calls for humility in leaders'. Vol 10, No 9, 6 May; p7.

PERKINS, S. J. (2003)

'Globalisation and HRM: partners in comparative perspective?'. *Journal of European Industrial Training*, Vol 27, No 9; pp461–72.

PERKINS, S. J. and HENDRY, C. (1999A)

IPD Guide to International Reward and Recognition: Diversity leverage and performance alignment in the transanational corporation. London: Institute of Personnel and Development.

PERKINS, S. J. and HENDRY, C. (1999B)

'International compensation', in: JOYNT, P. and MORTON, B. (eds) *The Global HR Manager: Creating a seamless organisation*. London: Institute of Personnel and Development; pp 115–43.

PERKINS, S. J. and HENDRY, C. (2001)

'Global champions: who's paying attention?'. *Thunderbird International Business Review*, Vol 43, No 1, January/February; pp53–75.

PERKINS, S. J. AND SHORTLAND, S. M. (2006)

Strategic International Human Resource Management: Choices and Consequences in Multinational People Management. London: Kogan Page.

PERLMUTTER, H. V. (1969)

'The tortuous evolution of the multinational corporation'. *Columbia Journal of World Business*, Vol 4, No 1; pp9–18.

QUINN PATTON, M. (2001)

Qualitative Research and Evaluation Methods. 3rd ed. Thousand Oaks, CA: Sage.

ROWLEY, C., BENSON, J. and WARNER, M. (2004)

'Towards an Asian model of human resource management? A comparative analysis of China, Japan and South Korea'. *International Journal of Human Resource Management*, Vol 15, No 4/5, June/August; pp917–33.

RUBERY, J. and GRIMSHAW, D. (2003)

The Organization Of Employment: An international perspective. Basingstoke: Palgrave Macmillan.

RUGMAN, A. (2000)

The End of Globalization: A new and radical analysis of globalization and what it means for business. London: Random House Business.

SCULLION, H. (2005)

'International HRM: an introduction', in: SCULLION, H. and LINEHAN, M. (eds) *International Human Resource Management: A critical text.* London: Palgrave Macmillan; pp3–21.

SMITH, C. and MEIKSINS, P. (1995)

'System society and dominance effects in cross-national organizational analysis'. *Work Employment and Society*, Vol 9, No 2; pp241–67.

THOMPSON, P. (2003)

'Disconnected capitalism: or Why employers can't keep their side of the bargain'. *Work Employment and Society*, Vol 17, No 2; pp359–78.

TRAXLER, F. and WOITECH, B. (2000)

'Transnational investment and national labour market regimes: a case of "regime shopping"?'. *European Journal of Industrial Relations*, Vol 6, No 2; pp141–59.

TREGASKIS, O. and BREWSTER, C. (2006)

'Converging or diverging? A comparative analysis of trends in contingent employment practice across Europe over a decade'. *Journal of International Business Studies*, Vol 37, No 1; pp111–26. Online version also available at: http:// www.palgrave-journals.com/cgi-taf/ DynaPage.taf?file=/jibs/ journal/v37/n1/full/8400174a.html [Accessed 15 June 2006].

TURNER, D. and NEWMAN, C. (2005)

'London ranked lower than its rivals in expat safety league'. *Financial Times*. 14 March.

VERNON, G. (2006)

'International pay and reward', in: EDWARDS, T. and REES, C. (eds) *International Human Resource Management: Globalization, national systems and multinational companies.* Harlow: Financial Times/Prentice Hall; pp217–41.

WHITLEY, R. (2000)

Divergent Capitalisms: The social structuring and change of business systems. Oxford: Oxford University Press.

WHITLEY, R. (2001)

'How are international firms different?', in: MORGAN, G., KRISTENSEN, P. H. and WHITLEY, R. (eds) *The Multinational Firm: Organizing across institutional and national divides.* Oxford: Oxford University Press; pp26–68.

WHITTINGTON, R. (2000)

What Is Strategy and Does It Matter? 2nd ed. London: Thomson Learning.

WILLIAMSON, O. E. (1975)

Markets and Hierarchies: Analysis and antitrust implications. A study of the economics of internal organization. New York: Free Press.

WORLD FEDERATION OF PERSONNEL MANAGEMENT ASSOCATIONS (2005)

Survey of Global HR Challenges: Yesterday, today and tomorrow. New York: PriceWaterhouseCoopers. Available at: http://www.wfpma.com/ PDFs/hrglobalchallenges.pdf [Accessed 15 June 2006].

WRIGHT, A. (2004)

Reward Management in Context. London: Chartered Institute of Personnel and Development.